ON CENSORSHIP

Joseph Brodsky 1940-96

INDEX ON CENSORSHIP 2 1996

Volume 25 No 2 March/April 1996   Issue 169

Editor & Chief Executive
Ursula Owen
Director of Administration
Philip Spender
Deputy Editor
Judith Vidal-Hall
Production Editor
Rose Bell
Fundraising Manager
Elizabeth Twining
News Editor
Adam Newey
Fundraising Assistant
Joe Hipgrave
Editorial Assistants
Anna Feldman
Philippa Nugent
Africa
Adewale Maja-Pearce
Eastern Europe
Irena Maryniak
Circulation & Marketing Director
Louise Tyson

Subscriptions Manager
Kelly Cornwall
Accountant
Suzanne Doyle
Volunteer Assistants
Michaela Becker
Thomasin Brooker
Laura Bruni
Nathalie de Broglio
Ian Franklin
Anne Logie
Nevine Mabro
Nicholas McAulay
Jamie McLeish
Albert Opoku
Lara Pawson
Grazia Pelosi
Dagmar Schlüter
Sarah Smith
James Solomon
Katheryn Thal
Saul Venit
Henry Vivian-Neal
Tara Warren
Predrag Zivkovic

Directors
Louis Blom-Cooper, Ajay Chowdhury, Caroline
Moorehead, Ursula Owen, Peter Palumbo, Jim Rose,
Anthony Smith, Philip Spender, Sue Woodford (Chair)

Council
Ronald Dworkin, Amanda Foreman, Thomas
Hammarberg, Clive Hollick, Geoffrey Hosking, Michael
Ignatieff, Mark Littman, Pavel Litvinov, Robert McCrum,
Uta Ruge, William Shawcross, Suriya Wickremasinghe

Patrons
Chinua Achebe, David Astor, Robert L Bernstein, Harold
Evans, Richard Hamilton, Stuart Hampshire, Yehudi
Menuhin, Iris Murdoch, Philip Roth, Tom Stoppard,
Michael Tippett, Morris West

Australian committee
Philip Adams, Blanche d'Alpuget, Bruce Dawe,
Adele Horin, Angelo Loukakis, Ken Methold,
Laurie Muller, Robert Pullan and David Williamson c/o
Ken Methold, PO Box 6073, Toowoomba West,
Queensland 4350

Danish committee
Paul Grosen, Niels Barfoed, Claus Sønderkøge, Herbert
Pundik, Nils Thostrup, Toni Liversage and Björn
Elmquist, c/o Claus Sønderkøge, Utkaervej 7, Ejerslev,
DK-7900 Nykobing Mors

Dutch committee
Maarten Asscher, Gerlien van Dalen, Christel Jansen,
Bert Janssens, Chris Keulemans, Frank Ligtvoet, Hans
Rutten, Mineke Schipper, Steffie Stokvis, Martine Stroo
and Steven de Winter, c/o Gerlien van Dalen and Chris
Keulemans, De Balie, Kleine-Gartmanplantsoen 10, 1017
RR Amsterdam

Norwegian committee
Trond Andreassen, Jahn Otto Johansen, Alf Skjeseth and
Sigmund Strømme, c/o NFF, Skippergt. 23, 0154 Oslo

Swedish committee
Gunilla Abrandt and Ana L Valdés, c/o *Dagens Nyheter*,
Kulturredaktionen, S-105 15 Stockholm, Sweden

USA committee
Rea Hederman, Peter Jennings, Harvey J Kaye, Susan
Kenny, Jane Kramer, Radha Kumar, Jeri Laber, Gara
LaMarche, Anne Nelson, Faith Sale, Michael Scammell,
Wendy Wolf

Index on Censorship (ISSN 0306-4220) is published
bimonthly by a non-profit-making company:
**Writers & Scholars International Ltd,
Lancaster House,
33 Islington High Street, London N1 9LH
Tel: 0171-278 2313 Fax: 0171-278 1878
E-mail: indexoncenso@gn.apc.org
http://www.oneworld.org/index_oc/**

Index on Censorship is associated with Writers &
Scholars Educational Trust, registered charity
number 325003

Second class postage (US subscribers only) paid at
Irvington, New Jersey. Postmaster: send US address
changes to *Index on Censorship* c/o Virgin Mailing &
Distribution, 10 Camptown Road, Irvington, NJ 07111
Subscriptions 1996 (6 issues p.a.)
Individuals: UK £36, US $50, rest of world £42
Institutions: UK £40, US $70, rest of world £46
Students: UK £25, US $35, rest of world £31

© This selection Writers & Scholars International Ltd,
London 1996
© Contributors to this issue, except where otherwise
indicated

Printed by Martins, Berwick upon Tweed, UK

Cover design by Andrea Purdie

Photo credits Front cover: *Der Spiegel*; Back cover and
title page: Joseph Brodsky (Jane Bown/Camera Press)

Former Editors: Michael Scammell (1972-81); Hugh Lunghi (1981-83); George Theiner (1983-88); Sally Laird (1988-89); Andrew Graham-Yooll (1989-93)

EDITORIAL

Arms and the people

STIRRING times in our own backyard. As we go to press the appeal against the expulsion of the Saudi dissident Mohammed al-Mas'ari is being heard. The deportation order came after strong pressure from the Saudi Arabian regime and British arms companies which are threatened with loss of trade. Al-Mas'ari is an Islamist whose bulletins are said to be reaching hundreds of thousands inside Saudi Arabia. Al-Mas'ari's own views are a challenge to our western democratic beliefs, but so too is the British government's threat to deport him. Or are we to be dictated to by one of the most repressive regimes in the world?

Al-Mas'ari's case coincides with the publication of the Scott Report on the sending of British arms to Iraq. What the inquiry reveals above all is the shocking extent to which the British political and administrative system now has the ingrained habit of telling its citizens as little as possible about politically sensitive subjects — in other words, that treats the public with contempt. Polls show that the majority of that same public is in no doubt that ministers and civil servants deliberately misled them and that the cover-up was to spare the government embarrassment. The government feared it would lose popularity if it was known to be condoning arms sales to Saddam Hussein. It seems a reasonable assumption.

Of course, *realpolitik* tells us that arms trading provides jobs and exports — and indeed that's another side of the debate the public was never allowed to have.

Meanwhile, British diplomats in former Yugoslavia seem primarily concerned that British arms manufacturers have not been winning contracts because of the ramifications of the Scott inquiry. However, as the UN embargo is lifted under the Dayton peace agreement, the British foreign secretary has done his bit by telling Slovenia that, if it wants to join Nato, it should buy British and other western European defence equipment. Never mind the images of war we've seen on our screens for more than four years, the desperate need for reconstruction in former Yugoslavia and western governments' failure to produce promised aid. As far as the arms trade and UK plc is concerned, it's back to business as usual. ❏

contents

Joseph Brodsky

24 May 1940 — 28 January 1996

JANE BOWN/CAMERA PRESS

Return of a poet

THE DEATH of a poet is not a death of personality. Poets do not die.
Administrative power — that embodiment of a craven world —
showed him many kindnesses and granted him great honours. But with all
that came the accusations of parasitism, exile to the West (a forced

mutation), and the refusal of a visa home to bury his parents.

I fear the 28th day of the month for my own reasons; these days, I shrink from it. The 28th is when things happen. A month ago, on the 28th, I flew home from New York. I called Joseph the night before. He said he couldn't seem to grasp an opportunity when it was there. The flight was cancelled. I called him again. 'See', I said. 'The fates are giving you a chance.' As it turned out, it was a chance they were offering not him, but me.

We talked about illnesses and operations and energies, and about the why and how of writing. And he repeated something he had once written — for Akhmatova, I think it was: 'The word is a commandment, a spell, a charm. The grand design. And it may save.'

Today, at dawn, I felt I saw him. It was as though angels or doctors were leaning over his body. 'Let us proceed...' 'But you see, I'd rather stay where I am. With him.'

He had always longed to be a footballer or a pilot, but his heart objected, fearful of the task. So he became a poet. They wouldn't even admit him back to the city where he was born to bury his parents. But then, he wouldn't admit the city — in its entirety — into himself.

It's always the 28th day. Especially 28th January in St Petersburg: Peter the Great died on the 28th; Pushkin died on the 28th; Dostoevsky died on the 28th; Blok completed *The Twelve* on the 28th, and burnt himself out writing it.

A poet doesn't die in death; he lives in the heart. Not the organ, the metaphor. His heart ceased to beat, it couldn't bear the burden. He had to make a choice: die with his own heart, or live with the heart of another. Everything rested with the heart. He might have taken the heart of a black racing driver killed in a crash. But he couldn't decide. The angels did it for him. They opened the way home, with his family there, in sleep. He died, and his own heart with him. The hungriest of Russian parasites is no more. We have seen the passing of a great sportsman and traveller. St Petersburg lost its poet. On the 28th... That was the day he came back to us. ❏

Andrei Bitov is a distinguished Russian novelist. His best known work is Pushkin House *(1978)*

Translated by Irena Maryniak

Elements of poetry

B RODSKY'S presence was a ballast to his colleagues in the poetic craft, and a point of reference. Here was a man who, through his life and work, constantly reminded us that, contrary to what we hear and read so often, there is such a thing as moral hierarchy. It is an absolute, proved neither in logic nor through discourse. Yet we affirm it daily, as we live and write. It has something to do with that elementary distinction between beauty and ugliness, truth and falsehood, compassion and cruelty, freedom and tyranny. But above all it indicates a respect for what is uplifting and a dismissal of — rather than contempt for — what is degrading. Brodsky's poetry fell into the higher category. His life reflected the heightened awareness which Pushkin observed in Mickiewicz: 'He saw life from a vantage point, beyond.'

In one of his essays Brodsky reflected that Mandelstam was a poet of culture. He too was a poet of high culture and thanks to this, perhaps, worked within the most profound current of his century, where humanity, threatened with the spectre of annihilation, discovered its past in the image of an endless labyrinth. As we descend into the labyrinth, we discover that if any good has survived from the past, it is thanks only to this hierarchy of moral distinction. The crazed Mandelstam scouring refuse for food in the gulag, is the very image of despotism and debasement, doomed to vanish. Mandelstam reciting his verses to fellow prisoners, is a heightened moment destined to last. Brodsky's verse was a bridge to the poetry of his predecessors — Mandelstam, Akhmatova and Tsvetaeva — built over a Russian language abused for decades. He was not a political poet, because he would not enter a polemic with an opponent scarcely worth the privilege. He engaged, instead, in the poetic craft as a form of activity unfettered by the tyrannies of time. ❏

*Polish-born poet and writer **Czeslaw Milosz**, (b1911) was awarded the Nobel Prize for Literature in 1980. He left Poland for exile in Paris in 1951 and, in 1960, moved to the USA where he took US citizenship in 1970*

Translated by Irena Maryniak

May 24, 1980

I HAVE BRAVED, for want of wild beasts, steel cages,
carved my term and nickname on bunks and rafters,
lived by the sea, flashed aces in an oasis,
dined with the-devil-knows-whom, in tails, on truffles.
From the height of a glacier I beheld half a world, the earthly
width. Twice have drowned, thrice let knives rake my nitty-gritty.
Quit the country that bore and nursed me.
Those who forgot me would make a city.
I have waded the steppes that saw yelling Huns in saddles,
worn the clothes nowadays back in fashion in every quarter,
planted rye, tarred the roofs of pigsties and stables,
guzzled everything save dry water.
I've admitted the sentries' third eye into my wet and foul
dreams. Munched the bread of exile: it's stale and warty.
Granted my lungs all sounds except the howl;
switched to a whisper. Now I am forty.
What should I say about life? That it's long and abhors transparence.
Broken eggs make me grieve; the omelette, though, makes me vomit.
Yet until brown clay has been crammed down my larynx,
only gratitude will be gushing from it.

Joseph Brodsky

Translated by the author

© *Reprinted from* To Urania: Selected Poems 1965-1985 *(Viking, 1988)*

A service of thanksgiving to celebrate the life and work of
SIR STEPHEN SPENDER
will be held on Wednesday 20 March at 3pm at the church of
St Martin-in-the-Fields, Trafalgar Square, London WC2

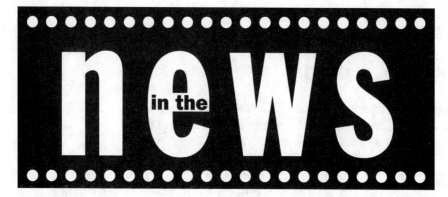

news

in the

- **poster poison** 'Too political' said the British Airports Authority of posters at UK airports offering advice to would-be immigrants and asylum seekers faced with the severity of the UK's harsher attitude to both — and banned them...

- **'cultural poison'** said the Vietnamese government of ads for western goodies and, until stopped by the investors it has worked so hard to woo, proceeded to paint out the offending slogans.

- **orange poison** More than 20 years after its release in 1972, Stanley Kubrick has personally authorised the release on video of his controversial film *A Clockwork Orange* (*Index* 6/1996).

- **winning the peace** The same media that fuelled the war in former Yugoslavia have put the weight of their columns behind the peace. 'But only so long as this remains the official line from the top,' comments our man in Croatia who remains sceptical of any sudden conversion.

- **meanwhile in belgrade** the government has taken over the country's only independent TV station, NTV Studio B...and in Sarajevo, the struggling independent TV station Studio 99 finds its freedom is less than absolute. And recently resigned prime minister Haris Silazjdic finds his views cannot get a hearing on national TV and radio.

• **fourteen russian journalists** have been killed in a year reporting the Chechen war.

• **thirty thousand dead** in civil war between government and guerrillas in Colombia in 1995, according to government estimates.

• **doctor zhang shuyun** is continuing her campaign to expose China's baby gulag (*Index* 4/1995). Adoptions and donations from the West, she stresses, are not the answer. The entire structure of state orphanages must be exposed and reformed from within.

• **twenty-one killed** and 100 injured in bomb blasts in Algerian capital. A town hall, and the national press centre named after assassinated journalist Tahar Djaout (*Index* 3/1995), were targets of car bombs on 11 February. According to *al-Ansar*, an underground news-sheet published in Sweden and close to the GIA (Armed Islamic Group), both attacks were the work of the latter's hard-core 'Death Squad'.

• **red alert** The China Film Bureau has refused to release certain politically incorrect films by Chinese directors for the Hong Kong Film Festival starting 25 March. Voicing its concern for artistic freedom after 1997, the colony's watchdog Arts Development Council admitted that for all its US$1 billion budget, it will be toothless when it comes to enforcement of its views.

• **black thursday** From Thursday 8 to Friday 9 February Internet users blackened their websites in mourning, in response to the new US Communications Decency Act, designed to clean up sex on the Net. Opponents of the act will challenge its efforts to 'set the ground rules for free speech in the twenty-first century'.

- **'free expression has gone into reverse'**, says the latest report from the Moroccan Association of Human Rights. Presenting its annual report on 17 February in Rabat, the association denounced the 'degradation' of human rights in a country where 'torture' and 'abuses of power' are still 'prevalent'. Thirteen people died in detention in 'suspicious circumstances' in 1995.

- **it was turkish journalists** from the national daily *Hurriyet* who planted their flag, that replaced the Greek's, on the island of no people, that Greece had invested with 'holiday homes' run under military auspices, that Turkey claims, that led to the Greek-Turkish flare-up, that caused the US to get its fingers burned in the latest Aegean rumpus. Nicole Pope adds from Istanbul: 'The nationalist media on both sides bear a heavy responsibility for whipping up a ludicrous, and wholly avoidable crisis.'

- **pity the poor journalist** According to a January survey, only 45 — compared with 56 last year — per cent of the French have any confidence in press reporting; trust in TV has fallen from 60 to 45 per cent. A bad day for democracy, comments Ignacio Ramonet in *Le Monde Diplomatique*, and blames the media's creeping take-over by big business.

- **deaths, arrests and disappearances** continue in Pakistan as government forces continue their onslaught on the Mohajir community in Karachi. The Mohajir Quami Movement, supported by reports in local papers, reports 12 dead in two nights of terror in the city on 15 and 16 February. Many more members or supporters of the MQM have been arrested or disappeared in raids on Mohajir localities.

- **asia's disappearing women** Pregnancy tests to determine the sex of a foetus have become a means of sexual selection in India, China and South Korea, where the abortion of female foetuses is reducing the female population at an alarming rate. At the present rate, reports *El Mundo* of Madrid, by the year 2000 there will be 70 million Chinese men condemned to celibacy for want of a woman.

• **by any other name** 'We would if we could,' said US State Department officials on the return of certain compromising documents confiscated in 1994 by invading US troops from the offices of the US-backed FRAPH. The Revolutionary Front for the Advancement and Progress of Haiti was responsible for the worst human rights abuses in Haiti following the coup that ousted President Jean-Bertrand Aristide in 1991. Officials said they felt the need to 'redact the names of known American citizens which appear in these documents'.

• **'nationalists of the world unite'** Europe is in danger of seeing the vacuum left by the collapse of Communism being filled by what it calls the Nationalist International, according to *Le Monde*'s editorialist. Reflecting on the penchant of French National Front leader Jean-Marie Le Pen for the likes of Russia's Vladimir Zhirinovsky and Iraq's Saddam Hussein, it warned against the growing links between reds and browns and the spread of racism in the 1990s. Le Pen was a guest at Zhirinovsky's flamboyant remarriage in an Orthodox church in February; at the start of the Gulf War he rushed to stand beside Saddam.

• **peace in indonesia** Twenty years after its brutal occupation of East Timor, the Indonesian government is vigorously applying the same techniques to 'pacifying' Irian Jaya for the greater convenience of the US conglomerate Freeport McMoran Copper and Gold who are extracting the local minerals. FMCG are accused of human rights abuses including torture and killings around the mine. They have also turned their skills to threatening journalists and intimidating newspapers back home that attempt to publicise the story.

• coups in waiting

WHEN Captain Valentine Strasser was recently overthrown in a palace coup by his second-in-command, most commentators believed it was because he was about to keep his promise and return Sierra Leone to democratic rule. In fact, his end had been foretold last November when he voted in favour of Nigeria's suspension from the Commonwealth in the wake of Ken Saro-Wiwa's execution. In a terse statement at the time, the Nigerian government made it clear that it considered governments in West Africa should have a better understanding of where their primary allegiances lay, especially those kept in power by Nigerian military muscle.

Such was the case in the Gambia, after all, where the current military leadership, installed two years ago, was loud in its support of their godfather. And now we hear, in quick succession, of a successful military coup in neighbouring Niger, a near miss in Guinea, and a likely coup-in-the-making in Burkina Faso where, according to Nigerian state broadcasting, Nigerian dissidents have been given 'military training camps' to launch an attack on the region's biggest and best-equipped army. On 22 February, an attempted coup was foiled in Benin.

• triumph over adversity

THE London-based Kurdish-language satellite television station MED-TV, has been the victim of Turkish government attempts to sabotage its broadcasts to some 35 million Kurds worldwide. Trouble began well before its first transmission hit the screens in May last year: disinformation campaigns, attempts to intimidate viewers in Turkey by destroying their satellite dishes, pressure on the UK government to withdraw its broadcasting licence and the use of state-of-the-art technology to jam live broadcasts were brought into play. None of this succeeded in preventing the station's output.

While some European companies have withdrawn their co-operation with the station for fear of jeopardising their business ventures in Turkey, the Turkish government's efforts to export their home-grown version of media repression against the Kurds has failed (see page 74).

• net note

THE year opened briskly for the rival exponents of control or freedom on the Internet. Battle was chiefly joined on sex and hate speech, already contentious areas in the conventional media in the West. In Asia, the desire to be abreast of the latest technology confronted more traditional attitudes to freedom of expression: 'not suitable for our cultural specificity'. China, naturally, led the way in control for anxious governments concerned to have it both ways. All of which we monitor in *Index Index* (see page 80-108).

Just one small anecdote to add. Determining that his fast-developing country was ready for Internet, and that he alone should be the one to sample its wonders, the president of Vietnam decided to install it in the privacy and security of his own palace. Only to be confounded when he was deluged with e-mail from disgruntled Vietnamese dissidents and exiles from around the world.

• an attack too far

EGYPTIAN actresses are striking back against Islamist strictures that have shrouded them from top to toe in black, inhibited their appearances on stage and screen, and made them the object of scurrilous attacks in the gutter press. The final straw was an attack on Egypt's most famous film star, Yousra, already the subject of a lawsuit lodged by Islamist lawyers who object to the exposure of her thighs on a magazine cover, and under attack for, among other film roles, her appearance in *The Immigrant*, a film by Youssef Chahine, himself a victim of Islamist attempts to ban the film as blasphemous. On 18 January, in the course of Egypt's celebration of 100 years of Egyptian cinema, actresses called a press conference at which they hit out at 'the present climate imposed by the dictatorship of Saudi Arabia and the fundamentalists [in which] a woman is a prostitute unless she proves the contrary by adopting the veil, and all actresses are seen as unbelievers.' Yousra, they added, was under attack for no other reason than that she was a woman.

• reluctant refugees

FEARS for the safety of 200,000 Rwandan refugees in Kibumba camp in Zaire are growing as government troops surround the camps and cut off supplies. The authorities in Kinshasa insist on the voluntary nature of the repatriation of the Hutu refugees but the pace of return — less than 200 on 13 February, the first day of the campaign for repatriation — is well below the UN High Commission for Refugees' daily target of 2,000. Clashes between the ill-disciplined and tiny force of 250 Zairean troops and the Hutu militias who are encouraging the refugees to resist repatriation could take a heavy toll. On 21 February, impatient at the lack of progress, Zaire ordered the UNHCR out of the camps because of 'their hostility to repatriation'.

Refugee camps in Burundi, however, are emptying fast as large numbers of the 70,000 Rwandan Hutus flee the attacks of Burundi's mainly Tutsi army.

• slide into genocide

ON 29 JANUARY, the 15 members of the Security Council invited UN secretary-general, Boutros Boutros Ghali to come up with proposals for avoiding a repetition of the Rwandan tragedy in neighbouring

Burundi by 20 February. The deadline has passed, and despite the secretary-general's repeated warnings, the international community had made no moves to deal with the rapidly spreading ethnic madness inside Burundi. As *Panafrika*'s editorialist indicates, many in the country think a genocidal war is now inevitable and are hastening to join their side. His is a rare voice among a partisan press whose incitements to hatred are all too reminiscent of the 'hate media' that fuelled the genocide in Rwanda.

'Each day, Burundi slides a little deeper into terror. In this day-by-day descent into hell, the voices of those who think violence is not the only way out of the crisis are gradually falling silent. Must we really believe that there is no sane person left in Burundi amid this madness that has taken hold of a whole nation? The last march organised by our women to protest the violence and the lack of justice was a fiasco.

Of the thousands of women expected, only a handful turned out to march in an atmosphere of general indifference. Have our sisters and mothers also picked their sides? The men of Burundi have become habituated to violence and death: news of fresh murders, further massacres comes in daily; these things have become so commonplace nobody bats an eyelid. As though it were normal; as though this were in the nature of things.

We are losing any sense of love and compassion. Each ethnic group is barricading itself behind its fear, its imaginings, its illusions and its hope that a leader — yes, a war chief — will come and rescue it. Those who do not share this vision of war are seen at best as naive; at worst, they are called traitors.

At *Panafrika* we are often asked where we stand on all this... At such times, we once more insist on our neutrality. *Panafrika* will always report things objectively as they are and open its pages to different voices and opinions. We believe that 'those who want peace work for peace.' Burundi is not necessarily doomed to destruction, there is no inevitable fate waiting to exterminate us. We must believe this if we are not to be sucked down by the madness that surrounds us.' Antoine Kaburahe, *Panafrika*, Bujumbura. ❏

MICHAEL FOLEY

Democracy courtesy Thomas Cook

MICHAEL FOLEY

A sensitive moment: Old City, Jerusalem

Eight hundred international observers pronounced the Palestinians' first election 'free and fair', but the media failed to come up to scratch

IT IS doubtful if there was ever an election more closely observed and monitored than Palestine's. Everywhere in East Jerusalem, the West Bank and Gaza, international observers were there to ensure that Palestinians were able to vote in a free and fair election without intimidation. The ink was hardly dry on the ballot papers before EU foreign ministers announced their satisfaction with the election and Yasser Arafat was being congratulated on his huge victory. The Palestinian people had experienced democracy.

There were muted references to some flaws in the process, but few suggested that lack of a free press and the extent of intimidation against newspapers and journalists might raise serious questions about just how free and fair the election had been.

Take Palestine's leading newspaper, *al-Quds*. Its editor, Dr Marwan Abu

Zuluf, regards it as the authoritative voice of Palestine, in the way *El Pais* might be of Spain, *Libération* of France or the *Guardian* of Britain. Last August following the publication of a statement from the Islamic group, Hamas, Abu Zuluf received a phone call ordering him to close. Four 'thugs', as he describes them, arrived to ensure that he did. If he had not, his vans would have been hijacked, he says with a resigned shrug. So when his night editor, Maher al-Alami, placed a story concerning Yasser Arafat on page eight and was summoned to Jericho on Christmas night and asked why he had not placed the story on page one, Abu Zalaf did not even report the incident in *al-Quds*. Alami was held by the Preventive Security Services for six days. Arafat personally ordered Alami's release. He is reported to have patted the veteran journalist on the head and said that if it happened again he was to dump some of the page one advertising. Arafat would pay (see page 73).

Such intimidation was not unique. *An-Nahar*, a pro-Jordanian newspaper, was ordered closed for the month of August 1994. It emerged with a new editorial line and even a new masthead, showing the Dome of the Rock, a very potent symbol for Palestinians. Asa'd al-Asa'd, the editor of *al-Bilad*, a new newspaper, does not fear Arafat. He is a novelist, a former president of the Palestinian Writers Union, and was imprisoned by the Israelis for publishing a banned cultural journal. He knows Arafat well, he says. Nevertheless this does not stop pressure being placed on him. He was contacted days before the election by 'Arafat's office' and asked to explain why he had not published any photographs of the chairman that morning. Asa'd tells the story to indicate how fearless he is and how he is above intimidation. The fact that such a phone call was made was taken as normal.

These lessons, and many more, were not lost on journalists. The press and broadcasting coverage of the election was cautious in the extreme. Instead of investigations and analysis journalists offered the public uncritical interviews, or a sort of public education journalism that informed voters about the election process, how to vote, who the candidates were and exhorted them to use their franchise. Broadcast journalists maintained that the two uninterrupted minutes of radio time given to every candidate on Palestine Radio was evidence of balance and impartiality.

The election was an advertising bonanza. Sixty-five per cent to 70 per cent of page one, and every page after that, was devoted to political

Palestine 1996: West Bank voters and the writing on the polling station wall

advertising in all newspapers. This, some journalists claimed, led to huge commercial pressures to produce the sort of journalism that would not threaten this financial windfall.

Meanwhile, in little villages outside Jerusalem, in small sports and community halls, candidates were grilled and questioned. There was no fear, no intimidation, just an exercise in democracy and the media had little or no role in it.

So if the media were not acting as watchdogs, who was? The international community, of course, in the shape of some 800 official observers for an electorate of 1.3 million. They were everywhere: sitting in at public meetings, investigating election education sessions, keeping an eye on classes for election officials. They filled in forms, kept notes and generally appeared serious and earnest. Most did not speak Arabic. They were recognisable in their blue shirts, blue sleeveless jerkins, with the EU stars, or the name of their country or organisation on the back. Alongside the official observers were an unknown number of the ubiquitous NGOs who wore blue baseball caps with 'NGO' emblazoned on the front. They were lawyers, consultants and researchers. With clipboards they questioned Palestinians, who have experienced occupation for nearly 30 years, about human rights violations. Observers squealed with delight when they bumped into somebody they had not seen since the South African, Mozambique, or maybe it was the Cambodian, election. Many had seen in democracy in all three. One English woman had notched up 11 elections.

The most famous observer was former US President Jimmy Carter. His arrival at Salah-din Street post office, one of the most sensitive polling stations in East Jerusalem, was high farce. Here was a man whose very presence was meant to be a guarantee of democracy who had such a security cordon of Israeli and American personnel that voting while he was around was nearly impossible. He did demand, successfully, the release of Palestinian observers detained by Israelis. But it did little good really. Throughout the day at Salah-din Street post office the Palestinian observers were ignored. Canadian and Belgian observers helped people vote if they could not read or write. It was they who spoke to the media. It was not until some US politicians noticed that one of the observers, a student, was pretty and spoke English that she was drafted in to stand beside the politicians while they looked concerned for Palestinian democracy with a real Palestinian. It was human rights tourism, or democracy by Thomas Cook.

So what about the journalists? Some will tell you that while there are about 400 journalists in Palestine, the reality is that only about 20 have the skills to produce newspapers, radio and television news with fairness and balance. Most have found it difficult making the transition from supporting the struggle for liberation to a commitment to democracy and the electorate. Palestinian journalists had little freedom of movement. They were unable to travel between Gaza and the West Bank. Travel between one town and another required going through Israeli checkpoints. They assumed they would not be allowed to publish anything critical of Fatah and Arafat. Most did not try. Hussein Daifallah of the Palestinian human rights organisation, Al-Haq, says that after 28 years of Israeli censorship Palestinian journalists are used to guidelines. Without official censorship they have imposed self-censorship. Even with serious press restrictions in law, Mr Daifallah blames the media itself. He will not accept that it will take time for a free press to develop. It was important for Palestinian democracy for the media to be involved and acting as a watchdog during this first election. They were not. ❏

Michael Foley *is media correspondent with the* Irish Times. *He was in Palestine with the International Federation of Journalists working on the IFJ's programme, Media for Democracy, with the Arab Journalists Association*

DIARY

ANDREI KOLESNIKOV

One day in the death of Pervomayskoye

On 15 January, after the six-day siege of Pervomayskoye in Dagestan, where Chechen fighters had been forced to take shelter with hostages from Kislyar, Russian troops stormed the village destroying everything in their path. Soon after these events, a journalist from *Moskovski novosti* describes a scene that has come to typify the brutal 15-month war in Chechnya

W^{E WERE} stopped at the check-point about 10 kilometres from Pervomayskoye. We felt reluctant to get out of the car: it was cold and windy outside and we'd warmed up during the two-hour journey from Makhachkala. But, of course, get out we did.

'Pervomayskoye? You must be off your head,' the OMON soldier[1] said, gloomily. 'What have you got?'

We began to rummage for our papers. He got even more upset. He said he needed a smoke. My colleague, Nail, offered him a light. The OMON man brightened up.

'I've seen foreigners with those. They work on kerosene. Are you going to make me a present of it then?' he asked. But he wasn't exactly shuffling his feet coyly as he said it. How could one refuse?

'My name's Gusein,' he said, relieved. We understood that the official end of things (which he too, evidently, found difficult) was over. 'All the journalists I've ever met pretend to be non-smokers. You're welcome to spend the night with me. Do you know how to get to Pervomayskoye? Do you really want to go? You know how many bodies they've got lying around there ?

We didn't.

IT's about three kilometres by dirt-track from Sovetskoye to Pervomayskoye. There are fields on either side, where until recently federal troops had taken up their positions. Now these have been taken over by kids from neighbouring villages, checking to see what the soldiers have left behind. And they've left a lot. The kids have divided the fields into sectors; better not trespass or you'll soon find yourself in the sights of a young sniper poised unsteadily under the weight of a *mukha* which he's just retrieved from the mud. The *mukha* won't shoot any more, of course, but that doesn't make things any more peaceful...

The kids say nothing as we approach but giggle nervously. Finally one of them puts a hand under his shirt with a sigh and extracts a linen bag with a stick of explosive inside. He hands it to us. We examine the contents and give it back. He shakes his head and, all of a sudden, runs off. Once he's well away, he turns and waves. It's a gift.

The eldest, aged about 12, stays behind, having apparently decided — magnanimously — to answer for everyone. He describes what they have found here over the past two days, shows us an unexploded mine which they have been contemplating a couple of hours without being able to decide whether to take it home or not. Then he complains that he had been in a hurry to buy a machine gun; he got it three days before the hostages came to Pervomayskoye. It cost 800,000 roubles. Where did he manage to earn that, we ask.

'I'm a collective farm worker,' he says, proudly, and laughs.

He complains that he doesn't have any cartridges. When he was buying the gun, he forgot about them. The soldiers who were here before the storming of the village had promised to let him have some, but once the storming started, they must have forgotten too.

We drive on and, close to the village itself, we see two exhausted, dirty, bearded Raduyev[2] look-alikes coming towards us along the road, with guns on their shoulders. Our driver puts his foot down on the accelerator in despair, because there's nothing else to be done. The car gets stuck in a pot-hole there and then.

The Raduyevs walk up and offer us a hand. We push and shove, and then we get chatting. It turns out that they are Avars from Sovetskoye, on their way home from a hare hunt. They have been hunting around Pervomayskoye all their lives, and nothing would prevent then from doing the same now. The hunt has been unsuccessful. They haven't come across a single hare. But they did find several bodies; they say exactly where. There was one sitting under a tree, just as though he were resting, they say.

We drive into Pervomayskoye. You couldn't mistake it: not a single house left standing. Not one. A ruined shell.

There are people swarming all around, trying to salvage what they can from the debris. But under this debris, there is more debris. In some places the pungent smell of decomposing bodies strikes the nostrils from below. The same smell issues from the trenches dug through the village. No-one dares approach them. Everyone is afraid they might be mined. Dead cattle litter the ground: cows, bulls, buffalo — dozens of carcasses. The village was far from poor.

In the centre of the village stands the ruined mosque. The erstwhile inhabitants of the erstwhile village gather here to discuss the latest developments. The main news has been circulating for some time. Every single villager survived the storming. A miracle.

Opposite the mosque stands the ruined house of the Imam's mother. And in the yard is the cupola of the mosque untouched by bullets and shell splinters. Another miracle. At first we thought it had been carried there whole by the force of the explosion. As it turned out, it had just been built from a pool of common funds, and they hadn't had time to erect it yet.

In one place the smell of rotting corpses was so strong that the villagers had decided to dig through the debris without the help of combat engineers. They got through it fast and found a head, then an arm and a foot. People came running. They were from Kizlyar, still looking for their relatives. One fell to the ground howling. He had recognised his brother by the sleeve of the anorak. They forced him up and made him look more carefully. There had been no mistake. Two gold teeth on the right.

They drove the brothers to Khasavyurt.

Just then a boy came running up to say that a group of Chechens had turned up at the mosque. The crowd tore over. It turned out to be two old men from a neighbouring village. The villagers surrounded them in silence. They spoke Russian.

The Chechens asked their neighbours' forgiveness and expressed their sympathy for them. They said that it would have been better if Raduyev had taken the hostages as far as their village, but that he hadn't been allowed to do so. The crowd was silent. The old men said that anyone left without a home could come and live in their village.

'We're all without homes,' somebody said.

'We'll take everyone,' the Chechen said.

'You know we won't come.' They told him. 'Why are you here?'

'We want to help.'

'Thanks.'

The old men left.

★ ★ ★

WE MET Abdurakhman near his former house, on the edge of the village, about a dozen metres from the former front line position held by the Chechen fighters. We already knew his story from others. We heard it in full from him.

On 9 January, when all the villagers left Pervomayskoye, he stayed behind because the cattle had to be fed.

Abdurakhman dug a trench in the yard of his house and hid there. He would crawl in at night, cover himself with a sheet of tin-plate and stay there until morning. It was very cold. Then the shooting began. His house was being destroyed before his eyes. The cow was still alive. He picked up a few things and some fresh bedding, and went to the mosque. He settled there as the storming of the village began.

He didn't like it much in the cellar, particularly as the fighters had put the bodies of eight of their colleagues there. They had brought them out of Kizlyar, as it transpired later.

He wasn't in the mosque for long. They started pounding it as well. After one direct hit the mosque caught fire. The old man moved into his son's house next door. There he found three hostages — two men and a woman. They were being guarded by fighters. He asked them if they were going to take him hostage too.

'No, grandad,' they said. 'Do what you like. No-one here'll survive anyway.'

The old man settled in his son's house. The storming continued. The hostages were taken away somewhere. One morning he was preparing himself a meal when a shell exploded inside the house and everything caught fire. Once again he survived.

The old man was at the end of his tether. He had nowhere else to go.

He found a piece of white rag — the remains of a bed-sheet — and walked straight down the street, assuming, quite correctly, that if he stayed alive he'd meet someone.

It was the last day of the storming. He survived and reached a group of Russian soldiers.

He told us that he wasn't planning to go anywhere: the cattle which had also survived needed to be fed.

His son came to find him. He had driven all the way from Ukraine when he heard what was happening. The old man refused to travel back with him.

'But Dad, you haven't got a house to live in,' the son bellowed.

'So we'll build one,' the old man said.

* * *

IT WAS dark and late. There was no-one left in Pervomayskoye; everyone had gone to spend the night in other villages. We drove to Khasavyurt.

'Found the bodies, then?' Gusein asked at the check-point.

'Bastard' said Nail, who had remembered the lighter, perhaps.

'I beg your pardon? Get out of the car!'

They kept us an hour and a half, and then we drove back to Moscow. ❏

Andrei Kolesnikov *is a correspondent for* Moskovskie novosti

Translated by Irena Maryniak from Moskovskie novosti, *4 February 1996*

1 Troops of the Interior Ministry
2 Raduyev was leader of the Chechen hostage-takers

MARTIN ADLER/PANOS PICTURES

Grozny 1995

'an internal
Russian matter'

Above: The much feared and rapacious troops of the Interior Ministry patrol the battered town
Left: Cigarettes, scavengers and survivors (John Spaull/Panos Pictures)

Above: A city lies in ruins and the world remains silent
Below: Living in darkness beneath the bombs

Above: Their house was destroyed before their eyes...mother and daughter comfort each other
Below: 'They demolished the flats in which I lived...see, that's it in the background'

Chechen warning

Seek not to know for whom the Chechen bell tolls write a number of correspondents in an open letter to *Le Monde* that taxes the international community with its pusillanimity on the war in Chechnya

'RUSSIAN military authorities say 50,000 — almost certainly an underestimate — have died in the Chechen war. Given the size of the population — one third or a quarter of that in Bosnia — and the fact that the war has gone on for only 15 months as against four years in Bosnia, proportionally the list of civilian deaths in the Caucasus vastly outnumbers that in the Balkans. It is a gruesome tally; everything is known yet silence reigns universally.

'The media desert grows. All honour to Sergei Kovalev, virtually alone among former Soviet dissidents in speaking out... Why do the killing fields of Chechnya leave the world's moral, political and spiritual leaders indifferent? What are public opinion and international institutions dreaming about? They tell us this is 'an internal Russian matter'. Maybe. But the friends of France would use their friendship to restrain her if she bombarded Corsica with tanks, helicopters and rockets. What an outcry if British soldiers treated Belfast in the same way as Russia dealt with Grozny: a five-week bombardment that reduced the town to rubble.

'What other European power would we allow to crush a province so brutally?... Imagine a group taken hostage by Palestinians; imagine the Israeli army acting in the same manner as the Russians in Pervomayskoye, destroying prisoners along with their guards, flattening from a distance an entire large village. A proper, and virtually unanimous, protest would resound round the world.

'Are not the citizens of Grozny, Goudermes, Chali, people of flesh and

Left: Mass grave of abandoned and unnamed corpses at the old cannery on the edge of Grozny (Martin Adler/Panos Pictures)

blood? Are there some places in the world where anything goes?

'Our taciturn and silent complicity, our sins of omission towards a people in danger, are not because of ignorance or a lack of imagination. They are the result of our fear.

'Russia is still the world's second nuclear power. This disturbs us. We would rather turn our backs...rather not imagine what other leaders in Moscow, madder or more determined than these, less controlled and increasingly uncontrollable, might do...

'Our rampant cowardice is unworthy of us. By giving the green light to the murderous generals in the Kremlin and the bellicose nationalist mood sweeping a country in disarray, we are adding one more link to a fatal chain.

'Europe is on the wrong track when it abandons the 30-50 per cent of Russians who are against the war to their lonely fate. It is coddling pan-Slavic aggression, overestimating its real power and preparing the way for its future triumphs and our disasters.

'The total inaction of the democracies is stunning. The negligence of the European Community and its Parliament is more frightening than shocking'

'The *spetnaz* [Russia's special operations commandoes] have been operating in Chechnya for a year. The total inaction of the democracies is stunning. The negligence of the European Community and its Parliament is more frightening than shocking. The vast silence of the planet is terrifying.' ❏

Vladimir Bukovski, Russian writer and former dissident
Daniel Cohn-Bendit, Euro MP representing Germany's Green Party
André Glucksmann, philosopher and writer
Czeslaw Milosz, Nobel prize-winning Polish writer
Peter Schneider, German writer
Susan Sontag, US writer
Jerzy Turowicz, Polish journalist and intellectual

24 January 1996

FABRICE ROUSSELOT

In search of the new republic

Lord Justice Scott's exposure of the secrecy and duplicity that characterised the UK government's arms deals with Iraq should have come as no surprise to a society in which, acording to a French journalist working in London, the 'culture of secrecy' is endemic and reaches out well beyond the confines of Parliament to operate as the most powerful form of censorship

I WAS not in London at the time so the story appeared even stranger than it might have done. Seen from Paris, the arrest of the ITV anchor woman, Julia Somerville, after the police had been handed snapshots of her naked child, seemed totally ludicrous. Even more incomprehensible was the decision of a Boots the Chemist employee to contact the police after seeing the pictures. In the end it took 10 days for a judge to decide not to prosecute and not to censor these pictures. But it was enough to put Julia Somerville on the front page of every UK tabloid.

To a foreign correspondent working in London, this story sums up the nature of censorship in the UK. Even if there are no 'censorship laws' as such, the UK has at its disposal a vast legal framework which allows the authorities to forbid or stop the publication or distribution of a lot of material — pictures, books, movies. The laws on obscenity or on the protection of children are cases in point.

According to civil liberties organisations, censorship in Britain is the most draconian in Europe. It affects not only editors or film and TV producers, but enters the everyday life of the average English man and woman — as Julia Somerville discovered. 'The main problem is that we don't have any declaration of human rights in Britain except one written in 1685,' says Connor Foley of the National Council of Civil Liberties.

'Therefore we don't have any freedom of expression. The government can intervene when it wants to stop what it wants.'

The power of government to intervene was demonstrated in the aftermath of the murder of the toddler James Bulger, killed by two 10-year-olds in Liverpool in 1993. Following their sentences of 'detention at the Queen's pleasure', the government decided to restrict the access of young people to certain types of violent videos. In his summing up, the judge said the two young offenders might have been 'influenced' by a video they had seen depicting a crime similar to the one which led to the death of Jamie Bulger. Despite conflicting 'expert' evidence refuting the causal connection between video nasties and violent crime, the restrictions imposed by home secretary Michael Howard are still in place.

The British Board of Film Classification is empowered to ban films and videos; restrictions on television are numerous. According to the code of conduct established by the Independent Television Commission (ITC), scenes involving nudity or sex 'should be reserved for broadcast after 9pm'. The same code establishes strict controls on 'bad humour' and 'bad taste'. Advertising is constrained by clauses determining 'public decency'.

As a result, there is a total absence of nudity in commercials. In France, on the contrary, there is no shortage of nudes in commercials — not that this is always relevant to the product or in the interests of the audience, but the decision to watch or not is left with the public.

The most striking thing about all this is the presence of a British establishment that considers itself the guardian of public morality and the arbiter of taste. It seems bizarre that the police have the power to decide what videos make suitable cases for prosecution: what qualifies them to be the censors of pornographic videos from Sweden or Denmark? Should it really be the government who decides whether or not the British public may view a channel like 'Red Hot Dutch'?

There are far more cut and censored films in the UK than in the rest of Europe; only Britain indulges in eccentricities like the *Lady Chatterley* trial; only in Britain would a director like Stanley Kubrick decide to censor by withdrawal his own movie (*A Clockwork Orange*) because he considered it unsuitable for this country.

Notwithstanding this 'moral censorship', some of the most powerful censorship in the UK is politically motivated. Under the Prevention of Terrorism Act, for instance, the British government has near absolute power to stop publication or transmission of everything it deems too 'sensitive' on Northern Ireland. From 1988-1994 the home secretary's Broadcasting Ban was used to ban many documentary films, books, songs and silenced even the voices of supposed IRA members and sympathisers, on the troubles in Northern Ireland.

Moreover, there is still the infamous 'D Notice Committee' that can challenge at will whatever it considers a threat to national security. Seen from France, the 'Spycatcher' case appeared particularly ridiculous. Here was a book documenting a conspiracy against a Labour government available everywhere in Europe except in the United Kingdom.

Over the years, British governments have developed a culture of secrecy that has now become a habit in day-to-day political life. The so-called 'cash for questions' scandal in which MPs agreed to raise questions in Parliament on behalf of particular interest groups or lobbies in return for personal cash payments, is one of the most blatant examples of voluntary censorship agreed on by the political class to protect its own interests. How is it possible for MPs to be paid for extra services or consultancies and the public kept in ignorance of something likely to influence the judgement of their elected representatives? Yet despite the recommendations of the Nolan Committee, appointed by the prime minister to clean up parliamentary ethics, MPs have refused to disclose their sources of income: collective self-censorship in protection of a common interest — and in defiance of the people's right to know. Even the prime minister went along with the MPs in defiance of public opinion.

Censorship is also used to cover up potential political scandals: anything threatening dangerous repercussions is not investigated. From Mark Thatcher's Middle East 'handouts' to the influence of the British government in the building of a controversial dam in Malaysia in which aid was linked to a substantial arms contract, it is difficult to unearth the real stories behind questionable government decisions.

It is incredible that the Mark Thatcher story has never been properly investigated. On several different occasions in the 1980s, Margaret Thatcher's son was accused of exploiting his position and taking a commission on a military contract worth billions between Saudi Arabia and the UK. The House of Commons looked into the matter only to decide to go no further. When *The Sunday Times* produced transcripts of alleged conversations between arms dealers and agents of the Saudi royal family apparently confirming that Mark Thatcher had acted as an agent in that deal, the British government observed that there was nothing new in the allegations and again refused to open an investigation. Was this because mother rather than son would have been the victim of an investigation that might demonstrate her abuse of the parliamentary 'code of conduct' that commits ministers to declaring conflict of interest between their public and private spheres?

FOR observers such as myself, censorship in the UK reveals a deeply conservative country still in thrall to its strict Protestant values. Not only does the state exercise powerful censorship, British society accepts, even demands in many instances, that it should do so. After four years reading the British press, the number of articles detailing calls from TV viewers complaining of the unsuitability of this programme or that at a particular time — before the 'watershed' hour of 9pm — still amazes me. These viewers do not present their personal opinions for discussion: most want simply to ban a programme outright, almost as if they were afraid of a real debate on the subject.

After four years in Britain, I am convinced that the powerful censorship operating in the UK is the outcome of the evolution of British society and politics over the last two centuries. Britain is the last country in Europe where society is still so strictly divided along class lines. Historically, the best way for the upper classes to do as they pleased was to keep the people ignorant or misinformed. This was as true in political circles as in everyday life. Subjects like sex, for example, remain taboo because the establishment has always used 'moral values' as a means of controlling the rest of the population.

It can be argued that the 1789 revolution not only changed French politics forever but also showed the French people that everything could be 'out in the open'. While things in France today are far from perfect, at least the knowledge that they once got rid of their royals gave ordinary people the sense that they could also force their governments to be more transparent in their leadership of the country.

As long as British society remains dominated by its class divisions or continues to tolerate the outrageous privileges of its royal family, it can expect censorship to remain as powerful as ever. ❏

Fabrice Rousselot *was London correspondent for* Libération *from 1991-1995*

JUDITH VIDAL-HALL

Scott, lies and misdemeanours

'TRUTH is a difficult concept,' said the head of arms sales at Britain's Ministry of Defence, Ian McDonald, and did not stop to hear the answer, 'Half the picture can be true,' from his colleague in deception, Sir Robin Butler, cabinet secretary and head of the Civil Service.

In 1985, at the height of the Iran-Iraq war, the foreign secretary, Geoffrey Howe, issued arms export guidelines saying Britain should not 'supply lethal equipment to either side' and should 'scrutinise rigorously all applications for export licences'.

In 1988 Saddam's final offensive against Iran had failed and the two exhausted countries settled down to an inconclusive ceasefire. British arms policy began to tilt towards Iraq; Howe's guidelines were secretly relaxed. But no-one was told.

In the meantime, Saddam had turned his weapons against his own people, killing 5,000 Kurds in a chemical attack at Halabja. But the West feared Iran's brand of Islam more than it loathed the butcher of Baghdad. And when Ayatollah Khomeini issued his *fatwa* against British writer Salman Rushdie, the tilt became a stampede by British arms dealers rushing to sell to Saddam. The guidelines became ever more flexible; government gave a nod and a wink to the arms industry. And still no-one was told.

It took the arrest and prosecution of a number of weapons manufacturers and the energetic action of customs officers in stopping what they considered 'illegal' arms exports to Iraq, to expose what many had suspected but failed to prove: the guidelines had become a sham. And still no-one was told.

By this time the government was only able to ward off growing embarrassment by authorising an inquiry. In 1992 Lord Justice Richard

Scott was appointed to get to the bottom of the affair. His report more than three years later is a damning indictment of the secrecy at the heart of government that enabled ministers to mislead and deceive Parliament and the people for so long.

The Scott Report is the most important constitutional document to appear in Britain this century. It exposes the lack of openness in government; the contempt of ministers for their constitutional responsibility to inform Parliament and the public of their actions and be held accountable for them; the plethora of so-called 'gagging' devices preventing access to government documents and the total lack of accountability within the Civil Service.

Above all, it exposes the contempt in which government, politicians and the bureaucracy hold the public. Scott is categorical: it was not 'national security' or the 'public interest' that caused government to engage in its tissue of deception and evasion: it was fear of 'public opinion' likely to condemn the cynical arming of a murderous dictator whose British weaponry had already murdered his own people and, only months later, would be turned on British troops in the Gulf War.

Time and again, when faced with direct questions in Parliament about policy on arms sales, ministers indulged in evasion, half-truths and downright lies. The list below details 24 separate occasions on which ministers lied — or at least struggled with the truth — before Parliament and colleagues. And it leaves us with a question for later: would a Freedom of Information Act have made any difference?

1989

January Trade minister Alan Clark to Tory MP Teddy Taylor: 'The guidelines are being kept in constant review in the light of the ceasefire and developments in the [Iran-Iraq] peace negotiations.' Tony Steadman, head of DTI's Export Licensing Unit, admits to Scott the answer is misleading.

April Chris Mullin, Labour MP, receives written answer to arms-related questions from Alan Clark, giving no indication of changed guidelines.

20 April Lord Glenarthur in House of Lords says exports to Iran and Iraq are covered by strict guidelines and scrutinised rigorously. (This was four months after relaxation in relation to Iraq)

20 April Alan Clark: 'Applications for such licences are examined against the guidelines on the export of defence equipment set out by the foreign secretary,

Sir Geoffrey Howe, in 1985...on a case-by-case basis, in accordance with stringent export control procedures which include, in particular, an assessment of the human rights record of the country concerned.'

21 April Prime minister Margaret Thatcher to Labour MP Harry Cohen says interpretation of guidelines is affected by end of Iran-Iraq war. Alan Clark in evidence says this shows she knew of the change in the guidelines.

21 April Thatcher to Cohen: 'The government have not changed their policy on defence sales to Iraq...'

3 May William Waldegrave, minister of state at the Foreign Office: 'The government have not changed their policy on defence sales to Iraq.'

8 May Lord Glenarthur reaffirms that 1985 Howe guidelines still in use. Mark Higson, Iraqi desk officer in the Foreign Office, tells Scott this is untrue and misleading.

June Howe replies to letter from shadow cabinet minister Peter Shore: 'We have not changed our policy on defence sales to either Iran or Iraq.' Higson admits this is wrong.

July Alf Morris writes to Foreign Office on behalf of Manchester Kurdish community to enquire on arms sales to Iran and Iraq. Assured neutrality of position by foreign secretary at the time, John Major.

8 August Letter from Waldegrave to Tom Sackville, Tory MP, says policy of impartiality operated towards Iran. Waldegrave admits to Scott that his letter gave a 'false impression' but that 'openness is not the only criterion.'

14 December Lord Trefgarne: 'We do not sell arms to Iraq...the sale of such items to Iraq or Iran is subject to very close guidelines.'

1990

18 April Trade secretary Nicholas Ridley tells House of Commons that government only 'recently became aware' of supergun. Sir Hal Miller makes 'embarrassing' disclosure to House of Commons.

5 December Tim Sainsbury tells MPs government 'scrupulously followed' official guidelines on exports to Iraq.

1991

31 January Major tells Sir David Steel: 'For some considerable time we have not supplied arms to Iraq.' Higson says Major knew or was misled by officials.

February Labour MP Tony Banks told by Alan Clark no Ministry of Defence official attended Baghdad arms fair, despite presence in Baghdad of Ministry of Defence official David Hastie, representing British Aerospace. Asked why

complete answer was not given, Ian McDonald, head of defence sales, replies: 'It was a complete answer... Truth is a difficult concept.'

1 July Archie Hamilton, armed forces minister: 'There were certainly no arms sales to Iraq from British firms. That is what I have always said and I confirm it absolutely.'

12 July Alan Clark denies giving 'a nod and a wink' to arms tools manufacturers over export licences, or that he had any knowledge of any equipment exported that was specifically for military purposes.

1992

30 January Shadow foreign secretary Gerald Kaufman writes to Foreign Office enquiring about arms sales. Major replies that 1985 guidelines still in force. Draft reply doctored.

May Junior minister Jonathan Aitkin: 'Since 1984 the United Kingdom has refused to supply any equipment which could prolong or exacerbate the Iran-Iraq conflict.'

12 November John Major: 'The suggestion that ministers misled the House is serious and scurrilous and has no basis whatsoever in fact.'

Late November Government assert that no change in policy occurred. This is because to admit a change would be to admit systematic lying to Parliament on the part of government ministers. 'Something that I was not aware had happened, turned out not to have happened' — John Major.

1994 Comments on misleading Parliament

9 February Sir Robin Butler, cabinet secretary and head of Civil Service, under questioning: '...one is often finding oneself in a position where you have to give an answer that is not the whole truth, but falls short of misleading.'

March William Waldegrave tells Commons Civil Service Select Committee that 'in exceptional circumstances, it is necessary to say something that is untrue to the House of Commons.'

5 April 'It is clearly of paramount importance that ministers give accurate and truthful information to the House. If they fail to do this, then they should relinquish their positions...' — John Major. ❑

Information supplied by Fulcrum Productions

Left: Lord Justice Scott by Peter Clarke

Lebanon 1980: all the news there was to read

Silence falls

**Their brief, but all too painful, encounter
with a critical, opposition press has
persuaded governments in the Middle East
to push the evil genii back into the bottle**

File compiled and edited by Eugene Rogan

EUGENE ROGAN

Rise and fall

FOR two years running Algeria has been the most dangerous country in the world in which to practise journalism. According to the Committee to Protect Journalists, a New York-based monitoring group, Algerians accounted for 24 of 51 press killings in 1995. Nor has the pressure eased in 1996: three journalists were shot, two fatally, in the first two weeks of January. It is the tragic end of a nascent critical press which emerged in the political liberalisation of 1989 only to be caught between the government and its opponents after the cancellation of parliamentary elections swept by Islamists in 1991.

While Algeria is the extreme case, it fits a broader pattern common to a number of Middle Eastern states in recent years. Through the 1970s, most of the Arab states were ruled by single-party regimes, or ruling families who exercised the same style of absolute government. Under such governments, where the press is an official organ of the state, newspapers and the broadcast media dedicate an inordinate amount of space and air-time to the trivia of colonels and kings, princes and presidents: reception of foreign dignitaries, pronouncements upholding state ideology, and compliments from abroad. The ruler reaffirms his enduring control by having his image placed prominently in the media each day — the photograph in the top left corner of the front page of newspapers, the first half of the televised evening news.

In many parts of the Arab world the authority of the ruler and the single party have gone unchallenged. There is no critical press in Libya, Sudan, Saudi Arabia, Syria or Iraq. Dissidents from those countries have sought asylum in the West to exercise their rights of free expression. As the recent case of Saudi dissident Dr Mohammed al-Mas'ari demonstrates, political exiles may well find their freedom of expression constrained when it proves inconvenient to host governments in Europe or the United States. Formerly, political dissidents found a more hospitable refuge in Lebanon where, up to the outbreak of the civil war in 1975, its press enjoyed the greatest measure of freedom and diversity in the Arab world.

Nor was Lebanon the unique centre of press criticism. To a lesser extent, the Kuwaiti newspapers were the most critical in the Gulf. Outside the Arab world, newspapers in Turkey and Israel could be privately-owned and intensely critical. However, the military is strong in both countries and could intervene with official censorship whenever the press trespassed into the domain of state security. The crackdown on the press in Turkey following the 1980 coup, and the sting operation conducted by Israeli secret agents to arrest Mordechai Vanunu for leaking the story of Israel's nuclear programme to *The Sunday Times* are cases in point.

In the course of the 1980s, a critical press began to emerge in a number of the countries of the Middle East such as Egypt, Tunisia, Jordan, Sudan, and Algeria. Its origins may be traced back to changes in the economic and political structures of the single party states. One of the defining features of such governments was the centralised planning of the economy. In the 1970s, state-led economies that had failed to foster sustained growth were being forced to restructure. State planners sought partnership with domestic private capital and foreign investors but, when they turned to international agencies to borrow funds, they were forced into austerity measures to trim national budgets to satisfy international creditors. Austerity provoked bread riots when government subsidies were cut, and private capital holders sought a say in political decision making to protect their investments from arbitrary state action. Economic liberalisation was followed by political liberalisation and the legalising of political parties, one consequence of which was the creation of an opposition press, breaking the state's monopoly over the media. Critical journalism was born.

Egypt and Algeria provide the best-known examples of these processes. Anwar al-Sadat led the way with economic liberalisation in 1974, IMF-inspired austerity measures, bread riots in 1977, and political pluralism in 1978, legalising both political parties and opposition newspapers. Events came later in Algeria. The first attempts at economic liberalisation date back to 1978, though the state only relinquished political controls in the aftermath of nationwide street demonstrations and riots against economic hardship and political corruption a decade later. President Chadli Benjedid's new constitution, enshrining political pluralism and economic liberalism, was approved by a national referendum in February 1989. The new constitution gave full scope to press freedoms, encouraging journalists from the state-owned press to launch independent papers. By the beginning of 1992, some 20 dailies and 50 weeklies were published in French and Arabic (*Index* Algeria File 4&5 1994).

Similar developments took place in Tunisia, Sudan and Jordan. Sudan's brief 'democratic period' of 1986-89 witnessed the creation of more than 35 political parties and some 40 newspapers (all subsequently closed in the aftermath of General Omal al-Bashir's 1989 coup). Following bread riots in Tunisia in 1984, economic liberalisation was succeeded by the re-emergence of opposition parties which began in 1987 to pressure the government for broader press freedoms. And in Jordan, the lifting of price subsidies in 1988 led to widespread rioting which led King Hussein to reconvene Parliament, hold elections, end martial law which had been in effect since 1967 and legalise political parties. In 1993, a new Press and Publications Law was adopted through which two independent dailies and some 20 party and independent weeklies were licensed.

These developments put Middle Eastern governments in a hard spot. At its most vulnerable, the Middle Eastern state was now held to account by a critical press. Where formerly the press had served as a reliable instrument to mobilise society on the state's behalf, now the press was making money out of allegations of government corruption and mismanagement. Some governments, working to draw in the reins before power slipped entirely from their hands, found the press the easiest target for the reassertion of control.

Across the Middle East, the critical press faces a range of repressive

News vendor Algiers; the press at a moment of peace in war

measures — financial, commercial, legal and extra-legal. Financial constraints take a variety of forms. Most controversial are state subsidies. Some of the wealthier states in the region have made sizeable investments in domestic and international Arabic newspapers on the understanding that these papers will never offend the patron state's sensibilities. At different times, Libya, the Palestine Liberation Organisaion (PLO) and Iraq have sponsored different Arab papers and magazines; since 1978 Saudi Arabia has become the dominant sponsor. Papers with sponsors survive, those without are driven to the margin.

Commercial pressures are also applied through advertising and sales. According to the Gulf-based Pan Arab Research Centre, some US$270 million was spent in advertising in Saudi Arabia in 1995, the largest single market in the Middle East. Newspapers which adopt a critical tone towards the Kingdom are banned not just from Saudi Arabia but from all the member states of the Gulf Co-operation Council. Many publications are entirely dependent on advertising revenues from the Gulf market. Access to market share for newspaper sales is also critical. Government-owned papers, produced under subsidised terms, are often larger and cheaper than non-governmental papers which have to survive by market forces or party subsidy. Thus, in Egypt, the government-owned papers have circulations in the hundreds of thousands, while opposition papers are lucky to sell in the low thousands.

The most direct form of censorship is through press laws. Often the first step in retrenchment following political liberalisation is the passing of a law to 'encourage a responsible press'. The most famous case at present is Egypt's Law 93 of 1995, though a number of countries have passed restrictive press laws recently:

• In Jordan, the Press and Publications Law of 1993 established clear restrictions to press freedoms forbidding news offensive to the royal family, to heads of Arab, Islamic or other friendly states, or to religions recognised in the constitution, as well as information about the armed forces or minutes of closed sessions of Parliament. The law does not provide for confidentiality of sources, which led to one correspondent's detention in September 1995 for his refusal to disclose the source for a story on Jordanian officials on the Iraqi state payroll [Salama Ni'mat, *al-Hayat*]. In its first two years, the PPL has led to over 40 court cases between the government and the press.

• In Lebanon, the press syndicate has lobbied to overturn repressive legislation established during the collapse of regular government in the civil war. Again, as in Jordan, the sensibilities of the president, prime minister and heads of friendly governments (particularly Syria) are required by law to be respected. A lack of such respect led to the conviction of the owner of the daily *as-Sharq* in November 1995 for publishing cartoons offensive to President Elias Hrawi and his wife Mona.

• In the newly-established Palestinian National Authority, Yasser Arafat made sure to draft a restrictive press law before having to share legislative authority with anyone else. The PNA is showing a remarkable level of repression for so young an entity; indeed many observers believe it is already performing like a mature single-party state in this respect.

What all these countries have in common is an electoral process that the ruling party seeks to dominate in the face of legal opposition movements critical of the government's performance. To this end it has sought to intimidate the critical press through a battery of repressive instruments. Middle Eastern states have made use of such instruments when facing critical votes. Recent instances include the extension of Elias Hrawi's presidential term for another three years in Lebanon in October 1995; presidential elections in Algeria and parliamentary elections in Egypt in November 1995; and Legislative Council elections in the PNA in January 1996. In each of these elections, the ruling power engineered favourable results and, to greater or lesser extent, the press was marked by a degree of self-censorship.

Intimidation is taken to its extreme in countries where the government or its opponents resort to extra-legal methods to intimidate the press. Journalists have been the target of beatings and torture in the Middle East as in many conflict zones. Of course the ultimate form of censorship is assassination. Two countries with the worst record for assassination of journalists in the Middle East are Turkey, where journalists working with pro-Kurdish and leftist publications have suffered the whole range of extra-legal violence, and Algeria, where the Islamist press has been banned and the secular press which continues to publish has been tarred by association with the state and is a target for the government's opponents.

Taken together, the pieces that follow highlight the vulnerability of the fragile experiment in press freedoms which the region has witnessed in recent years. Yet the authors, all practitioners who have contributed in their own way to the watchdog role the press aims to play over state and society, remain optimistic. Perhaps the critical press, once released, is not so easily forced back into a bottle. ❏

Eugene Rogan lectures in the modern history of the Middle East and is a fellow of St Antony's College, Oxford

ABDUL BARI ATWAN & JIHAD KHAZEN

In the Saudi pocket

*T*HE *Saudis are not the first to invest in the Arab media. An international Arab press has existed under foreign patronage since the last century. From the 1970s, the migrant Arab press began to take on additional significance. Initially under Lebanese control, this migrant Arab press has at different times been sponsored by the PLO and the governments of Libya and Iraq. Their publications were politically informed and, by and large, unsuccessful. Not so the Saudi-sponsored press. It has employed the latest technology and hired the most respected journalists to produce newspapers and magazines on a par with those published in the West. But at what cost?* **Jihad Khazen,** *editor of the top-selling daily al-*Hayat *(Life) and* **Abdul Bari Atwan,** *editor of the struggling independent daily al-Quds al-Arabi (Jerusalem), both London-based, argue the toss*

AL-QUDS AL-ARABI

Abdul Bari Atwan

Abdul Bari Atwan A quick look at the map of the Arab media shows that the Kingdom of Saudi Arabia dominates 95 per cent of the Arabic-language newspapers and magazines, radio and television stations in the Arab countries and abroad. This domination is either direct, such as total ownership by members of the royal family and their relatives, or indirect.

The Saudi desire to dominate the Arab media may be traced back to the propaganda war conducted by Gamal Abdel Nasser in Egypt against the Saudis in the 1960s, and the tremendous wealth generated by the oil booms of the 1970s. Under the guise of moderation, the Saudis began in 1978 to acquire a media empire to combat revolutionary ideologies (Communist, Arab nationalist or Islamist) and to stifle any criticism of the Kingdom and its ruling family. This allowed the Saudis to set the rules for press coverage of their affairs, both through the press they owned and the power of their massive wealth over the domestic press of other Arab countries.

The Saudi government signed 'media protocols' with the ministries of information of several Arab states, including Egypt. Under these protocols, the publication of any material critical of Saudi Arabia and its internal situation and the domination of its affairs of state by the princes and their acquisition of public funds was prohibited. One Egyptian editor-in-chief said he had received clear instructions from the Egyptian ministry of information not to criticise either King Fahd, his government, his family and his policies or the Egyptian president, Hosni Mubarak, and his sons. Criticism of anything else was permissible.

Through its dominant position in the Gulf Co-operation Council, Saudi Arabia was able to impose its media policy on the smaller Gulf states. It was instrumental in getting the Conference of Gulf Ministers of Information to issue resolutions to ban the few newspapers and magazines that attempted to criticise it, and to blacklist and isolate certain writers and journalists, prohibiting any dealings with them whatsoever.

Facilitated by the entry of Egypt and Syria into the coalition, the efficacy of the Saudi media empire and the role it is intended to play became abundantly clear during the [Second] Gulf War when it succeeded in preventing the expression of views other than those of the anti-Iraqi coalition. In Saudi Arabia the media is like a veiled woman. Beneath the veil you may have the finest dressing — the best technology, the best writers and journalists, the finest offices. But it is veiled, completely covered in black. It is censored.

Jihad Khazen The Arabic press has very different characteristics from the western press, the two chief distinctions being the relatively limited financial resources and the very limited freedom of the Arab press. Limited resources have resulted in a system of patronage.

Compared to papers in the West, Arabic newspapers also have limited circulations. Only in Egypt, with its large and urbanised population, do national newspapers enjoy circulations in excess of 100,000 copies. *Al-Ahram* (The Pyramids) and *al-Akhbar* (The News) both sell over 500,000 copies of their daily editions and more than one million copies of their weekend editions. However, in most Arab countries national newspapers sell no more than between 5,000 and 10,000 copies a day. Revenues from sales as well as advertising are a fraction of those in the West.

Estimates made recently by a subsidiary of Saatchi & Saatchi put total advertising expenditure for 1994 in the Gulf and other important Arab press countries such as Jordan, Lebanon, Yemen, Egypt and Morocco, in the region of US$900 million, a meagre one third of one per cent of global advertising, which totalled US$330 billion. Advertising in Israel alone reached nearly US$800 million in the same year.

Saudi Arabia's role as sponsor of the Arab press results from its position as the country where almost all advertising in the Arab world is concentrated. Industrialists from Boeing in Seattle all the way to Datsun and Toyota in Japan are all interested in the single Saudi market. Their advertising budget is allocated in proportion to a newspaper's sales in the Kingdom. Without the Saudi market al-Hayat could not survive. It sells all over the Arab world except in Iraq and Libya. It earned about US$13 million in advertising revenues last year, of which US$12.5 million came from Saudi Arabia.

This holds for the international Arabic press in general. Two years ago, probably under pressure from the 'ulama [religious establishment], the Saudi information minister decided to ban all women's magazines. The next day, 19 out of 24 magazines folded because they were dependent on the Saudi market for advertising. The only way to survive is to sell more copies in Saudi Arabia and get more advertising. The sponsorship is really indirect.

I don't mind my paper being banned anywhere for one day — in fact it's good publicity to show that we are not toeing the line of this Arab government or that. But when the ban is indefinite, particularly in Saudi Arabia, it can be really dangerous. We were once banned indefinitely by Saudi Arabia. It lasted 20 days and cost us nearly US$1 million. Had we been banned for another month or two we might have folded. Not only did we lose 21 days' advertising but we lost ads that were part of campaigns: banned in February, we lost advertising right through April.

If we are going to be banned in Saudi Arabia I have to make the decision myself. I want to know if this one line in an editorial is worth US$40,000. We consciously went after stories that got us banned. We interviewed Iraqi foreign minister Sahhaf last year and were banned. We interviewed the Iraqi oil minister and were banned. I told my staff to go after the story because it was worth the US$40-50,000.

Despite all the problems, we never ever publish a story on request. We commit sins of omission. There was a very important story about an Egyptian doctor arrested in Saudi Arabia which heightened tensions between the two countries. I refused to take the line of the Egyptians or the Saudis. Rather than risk alienating two of the most important countries for the paper I ignored the whole story. No-one forced my hand, but I couldn't put what I wanted in the paper.

Jihad Khazen

Atwan The Saudis dominate the press in a number of ways. Their newspapers have become very influential — the importance of a story is confirmed only if it appears in the Saudi-sponsored press. One day I was called by the BBC-TV Arabic Service: 'There's a story on your front page today, saying such and such. Is it true?' I asked why he should doubt it and he replied: 'It's not published in *al-Hayat* or *al-Sharq al-Awsat.*'

They definitely want to cover up their domestic affairs. The Saudi press doesn't discuss anything about Saudi Arabia. No-one has any sense of how many people are in prison or any statistics on road accidents for fear that such reporting might be construed as a criticism of the king or his government. Saudi newspapers don't talk about Saudi affairs, Arab newspapers don't, British newspapers don't, so who does? The British in particular are intimidated by the Saudis. UK foreign secretary Malcolm Rifkind used his first meeting in Saudi Arabia recently to criticise Mohammed al-Mas'ari. Who is Mas'ari? Rifkind did it because the Saudi authorities are upset about a Saudi opposition movement in Britain.

Princes of the Media

Saudi Research and Marketing Company Incorporated in 1978, the London-based SRMC currently publishes over 15 daily, weekly and monthly publications, chief among them the green-paged daily, *al-Sharq al-Awsat* [225,000cc], and the political weekly *al-Majalla* [120,000cc]. The organisation is owned by Prince Salman bin 'Abd al-'Aziz, sixth in line to the Saudi throne; the chairman of the board of directors is his son, Prince Ahmad bin Salman. All SRMC editors-in-chief are Saudi nationals.

Al-Hayat Press Corporation Based in London with branches in Riyadh, Jeddah, New York and Paris, the corporation publishes the influential Arabic daily *al-Hayat* [110,000cc], edited by Jihad Khazen, a Lebanese of Palestinian origins, and a political weekly magazine, *al-Wasat* [100,000cc], edited by another Lebanese national, George Sim'an. Since 1990 the corporation has been owned by Prince Lt Gen Khalid bin Sultan bin 'Abd al-'Aziz, who served as commander-in-chief of the Arab forces in the Gulf War.

Middle East Broadcasting Centre Created in September 1991 by Saudi billionaire Salih Kamil, the London-based MBC was the first Arab satellite TV station. It broadcasts to Europe and the Middle East. It was bought in 1993 by Walid and 'Abd al-'Aziz al-Barahim, brothers-in-law of King Fahd and uncles

We are banned in Saudi Arabia and, as a result, are completely deprived of advertisements. The last meeting of Gulf information ministers decided to ban any Arab newspaper critical of any of the Gulf Co-operation Council countries. There was only one newspaper banned: *al-Quds*.

To shape a paper around a market that represents some two per cent of the Arab people is disastrous. We would like a paper that caters for the whole of the Arab world, for the 98 per cent. As journalists we have championed freedom of expression and freedom of the press. If, as in Saudi Arabia, you cannot question a minister, nor talk about women driving cars, nor about commissions and corruption, if you can't talk about deals for arms that are never used, then what is the purpose of journalists here? We don't have as much at stake as *al-Hayat*, we don't publish 50,000 copies, but sometimes you lose your pride, sometimes you lose your principles. I wouldn't want to be editor of *al-Hayat*. At least I can say we are 95 to 96 per cent independent. And we have the freedom to of the king's youngest son, Prince 'Abd al-'Aziz bin Fahd, counsellor at the Royal Palace with ministerial rank. It is rumoured that the Saudi monarch is the real owner of MBC with first and last say in the management of its affairs. The channel is free to viewers.

Arab Media Corporation Owns the Rome-based Arab Radio and Television (ART) network, which is set to expand from its current four satellite TV channels to 14. Co-founded by Salih Kamil, who is said to own up to 90 per cent of AMC, and a nephew of the king, Prince Walid bin Talal bin 'Abd al-'Aziz, who reportedly owns some 30 per cent of the shares in ART. Prince Walid is also connected, through a 4.1 per cent shareholding in Mediaset, to the Fininvest Group of Silvio Berlusconi.

Orbit Television A subscription satellite TV network of 28 chains based in Rome and broadcast to 23 countries, Orbit is owned by Prince Fahd bin 'Abdullah bin 'Abd al-Rahman, a nephew of King Fahd. The network is rumoured to be losing money in its competition with rival MBC. In June 1994 Orbit concluded a contract to transmit the BBC Arabic Service television. The network provoked a storm of criticism in January 1996 for censoring all BBC coverage of Saudi dissident Mohammed al-Mas'ari's controversial extradition order. **ER**

write any story tomorrow.

Khazen This is really the problem. You can publish and be damned and sell to a few friends and a few Arabic readers in London and Paris; or you can be more careful and sell to a number of Arab countries; or be even more careful and sell to all of them — and not have a newspaper. You have to draw a line somewhere. *Al-Quds* definitely has more touchy stories than *al-Hayat*, but as a result it sells in five or six countries while we sell in 18 out of 20. We are totally free to support or oppose the peace process, but we have to be very careful talking about Saudi domestic affairs or religious matters. I don't know what is better. It's a personal decision more than anything else. ❏

*Abdul Bari Atwan is editor-in-chief of al-Quds al-Arabi; **Jihad Khazen** is editor-in-chief of al-Hayat. Both Arabic daily papers are London-based*

SALAH ELDIN HAFIZ & EUGENE ROGAN

Press law 93, 1995

After a period of relative freedom, Egyptian journalists are threatened by a retrograde new law

IN FEBRUARY 1996 the Egyptian Organisation for Human Rights issued a timely report, *Journalists Behind Bars*, which examined the implications of new press legislation on Egyptian journalists. According to their research, 13 journalists have been convicted and sentenced to fines and prison terms in recent months; another 16 are currently under investigation or awaiting trial. Those charged include some of Egypt's best-known opposition journalists, including the editors-in-chief of the Islamist paper *al-Sha'ab* (The People), the Liberal Party paper *al-Ahrar* (The Liberals), and the nationalist paper *al-Wafd* (The Delegation). Most have been accused of libel for allegations of corruption against public figures. To date, no major case has involved journalists from the state-owned press. One can only conclude that the government is using new press laws to divide the profession and to intimidate the opposition papers into adopting the tone of the national press.

Press freedom and political liberalisation have gone hand in hand in Egypt. Gamal Abdel Nasser made Egypt a single-party state and, in 1960, nationalised the press. His successor, Anwar al-Sadat, reintroduced political parties in 1976 and with them the beginning of an opposition press. Sadat put distinct limits on political and press liberties, notably in the creation of a government-appointed watchdog, the Higher Press Council (1975) and, in 1980, the Press Authority Law which reaffirmed state ownership of the 10 national press organisations.

The government under Hosni Mubarak may be divided into two camps: one which views democratisation as the main achievement of his rule, exemplified by freedom of expression; and a hardline camp which believes the Egyptian press has gone beyond its limits for the past decade and that, while one can keep talking about democracy, the press needs to be brought under control.

On 27 May 1995, the hardliners prevailed. Without consultation or prior debate the Egyptian Parliament passed draconian new press legislation, Law 93 of 1995. Four thousand journalists of both the government-owned newspapers and the opposition press converged in a series of extraordinary sessions of the Press Syndicate's council to express outrage at the reversal of both the fragile democracy movement and freedom of expression. Many journalists viewed the timing of the legislation as too close to the November parliamentary elections to be coincidental. The critical press is outspoken in its attacks on government figures it suspects of political corruption, lack of ethical standards, misappropriation of public funds and undemocratic behaviour. This could have proved embarrassing during an electoral campaign in which the government was intent on sweeping the polls.

Journalists were left in no doubt that Law 93 was designed to muzzle them through intimidation. It was now an offence to publish stories 'deriding government officials and institutions', a vague and ill-defined term which could be applied to virtually every opposition daily's front page. The law allows for stiff punishments of up to five years' imprisonment and fines of up to LE20,000 (US$5,650) for 'publication of false news that is harmful to state interests'. Worse yet, Law 93 eliminates previous legal guarantees against preventive detention of journalists: state prosecutors may now take journalists into custody while they are still under investigation.

In response to this frontal assault, the Press Syndicate called on the government to cancel the law within two weeks or face a general journalists' strike, unprecedented in Egyptian history. They were supported by a number of political parties and civil organisations, and more than 30 international organisations including Amnesty International, Article 19, and Reporters sans Frontières.

Faced with co-ordinated domestic and international opposition, Mubarak defused the crisis in a six-hour meeting on 21 June with the Press Syndicate council in which he agreed to convene a committee to produce a revised and comprehensive press law within three months. The committee would be composed of members of the Press Syndicate, the Higher Press Council, and various legal experts. Mubarak also responded to opposition papers' complaints of lack of access to government information by ordering ministries to make 'authentic information' available to all journalists, government and opposition alike.

The strength of the journalists' position was reinforced by the fact that the press did not divide into government- and opposition-owned camps. This unity seemed threatened when the composition of the new press law committee was announced in mid-July. Of its 30 members, seven came from the Press Syndicate's council and 12 from the government-appointed Higher Press Council. There were also 11 non-journalist public figures and legal experts. Representatives of the opposition press were completely excluded from a committee that included many advocates of restrictions on press freedoms. Few could doubt the intentions of the new committee when one of its legal experts, Shawki al-Sayed, threatened to file a libel suit against the editor of the opposition paper *al-Wafd*, Gamal Badawi, for publishing an article criticising the composition of the committee and al-Sayed's appointment in particular. In the event, the suit was dropped and four journalists known for their opposition to Law 93 were added to the committee.

Between July and October, the new committee met only twice for a comparative discussion of the press laws of other nations, without broaching the subject of Law 93 itself. The government was accused of foot-dragging and the committee began to look like a diversion to distract journalists' attention while the government proceeded with election strategies.

A number of draft laws and recommendations were put forward to assist the committee in its deliberations. The Legal Aid Centre for Human Rights, an Egyptian NGO, drafted a press law in August; the Third General Press Conference produced 40 recommendations in September; and the Press Syndicate approved its own draft law of 64 articles on 24 December.

The Press Syndicate's draft seeks to protect journalists from government pressure by rejecting imprisonment and limiting fines to a maximum of LE2,000. It also calls for the lifting of all restrictions on the publication of newspapers and the elimination of all types of censorship. It is unlike anything that the government-appointed committee is likely to produce.

Meanwhile, journalists were targets of legal and extra-legal intimidation. Editor Gamal Badawi was forced off the road and beaten by 10 men who later issued a statement linking the attack to the critical editorial line on Law 93 taken by his paper, *al-Wafd*. And, in spite of

National and opposition press in Egypt

CURRENTLY, two kinds of newspapers are published in Egypt: the national or state-owned newspapers and the newspapers established by the opposition parties. The latter include an entire spectrum ranging from the Marxist left through the traditional liberal papers to the Islamic right. The opposition press enjoys greater freedom to criticise and attack the government than the state-controlled press. The state-owned media, however, enjoys exclusive access to official news, which is denied to the opposition press because of its alleged tendency to distort facts which detracts from its credibility and confuses the public.

THE NATIONAL PAPERS
Al-Ahram (The Pyramids), founded in 1875, with a domestic daily and Arabic international edition published by satellite in London, Frankfurt and New York, as well as French- and English-language weeklies. Circulation 1,000,000
Al-Gomhouriya (The Republic), circulation 650,000
Al-Akhbar (The News), circulation 789,268

THE OPPOSITION PRESS
Al-Ahali (The Peoples), leftist Tagammu Party
Al-Ahrar (The Liberals), Liberal Party
Al-Arabi (The Arab), Nasserist Party
Al-Sha'ab (The People), Islamist-oriented Labour Party, circulation 50,000
Al-Wafd (The Delegation), Wafd Party, circulation 260,000 *ER*

assurances from the government that the press law would not be applied pending the committee's drafting of new legislation, several journalists were charged under Law 93. In October, Magdi Hussein, editor of the Islamist-oriented *al-Sha'ab*, was charged with libel by Alaa al-Alfi, son of the interior minister. The story, by an anonymous reporter, referred to an altercation over non-payment of a dinner bill by the son of a government minister, both unnamed. Al-Alfi challenged the veracity of the article (and incriminated himself) by producing a paid dinner bill, even though Hussein reminded him that the article mentioned no names. Hussein was found guilty in January 1996 and sentenced to one year's hard labour, a LE15,000 fine, and LE500 in damages to al-Alfi. The prison term has been suspended though Hussein faces a second libel suit, along with two other defendants from the opposition press, for alleging that a victorious parliamentary candidate had hired thugs to intimidate voters at the polls.

The indomitable Gamal Badawi was the second to be charged, this time by an outgoing member of parliament for allegations of misuse of state property. Abdel-Aal al-Baqouri, editor of the leftist Tagammu party organ *al-Ahali* (The Peoples) and a member of the state-appointed committee to draft a new press law, was sentenced *in absentia* to two years' imprisonment and LE50,000 in fines and damages for printing allegations of influence-peddling by a police brigadier.

The common theme running through these cases is the conduct of parliamentary elections. By all accounts the elections were marred by violence and irregularities at the polls. According to the Centre for Human Rights Legal Aid in Cairo, some 51 people were killed and 878 wounded in election-related violence. Even government officials were forced to acknowledge that some candidates had stormed polling stations and rigged the vote and that, in the words of Major-General Mohammed al-Menshawi, director of the election department of the Ministry of Interior, 'a limited number of violations' were committed by security forces. The result was the most heavily pro-government Parliament since the reintroduction of multi-party elections. The ruling National Democratic Party won 317 seats outright, and of 113 so-called independents some 99 crossed the floor to rejoin the NDP, which left the government with 416 seats in the 444-member People's Assembly. Perhaps the only positive thing that can be said about the elections was that these violations were reported in the Egyptian press.

Egyptian journalists await the March deadline for the government-appointed committee to present a revised press law with some pessimism. They do not expect liberal legislation to emerge from the committee and are not confident of a sympathetic hearing of their views before the new Parliament when the revised draft is presented for debate. As one leftist journalist explained: 'What we fear is that they will take our law [ie the draft prepared by the Press Syndicate] and the law prepared by the government-appointed committee and come up with something totally different from what we want.' ❑

Salah Eldin Hafiz is managing editor of the Egyptian daily, al-Ahram *and prize-winning author of books on press freedom and democratisation in Egypt*

CAROL HAKIM

Lament for Beirut

Fifteen years of civil war cost Lebanon its pre-eminent position in Arab journalism

THERE was a time in the 1960s and 1970s when Beirut boasted the freest, most dynamic press and publishing scene in the Arab world. Constitutional guarantees, a liberal intellectual environment and abundant capital fostered the freedom of expression denied elsewhere in the Arab world and attracted writers, intellectuals and dissidents from other Arab countries. Through the papers and periodicals they founded, as well as their contributions to the existing Lebanese press, they created a centre of debate on issues, events and ideologies of concern to the entire region. It was the Lebanese press that kept the Arab world informed about itself; its influence extended through the region.

However, the expansion of the press was not reflected in the quality of its journalism: standards of reporting as well as ethics took second place to passionate polemic and propaganda; party loyalty or the interests of backers — many papers survived on subsidies from other Arab countries — left little room for dispassionate analysis or factual information. Yet there was a sense in which multiple propagandas and competing regional ambitions cancelled each other; what could not be found in one paper, backed say by Libya, would be given prominence in another backed by Syria. All in all, there was more news coming out of Beirut than from any other Arab capital then or since.

When war broke out in 1975, rival sectarian militias, the PLO and the Syrians imposed control on 'their' publications by force. Methods included behind the scenes political pressure, threats and physical intimidation, kidnapping and assassination of journalists as well as the bombing of newspaper offices.

Human and material losses were massive: 25 Lebanese and 12 foreign journalists were killed and many more injured. From 1976, attacks against press offices forced many periodicals to close and journalists to emigrate, mostly to Paris and London. Few competent journalists remained.

Those who did remain adapted to wartime conditions: chose a side and came to terms with the demands of those in power. Factional and highly partisan newspapers, supported by the guns and money of their patrons, multiplied and thrived. In the increasingly fragmented state, with the country physically divided into the fiefs of warring factions, newspapers published in one region were frequently unable to distribute in 'enemy' territory. Persistent intimidation paid off: the press resorted to protective self-censorship. Gradually, and often through a painful process of trial and error, it discovered the limited room for manoeuvre and learned to play by the rules. The surviving remnants of the independent and objective press confined itself to factual accounts that attempted to make sense of often conflicting and unrelated events. Short on critical analysis or editorial comment, they employed allusion and metaphor to make a point.

Changes in the official press laws compounded the unofficial censorship imposed by the war. In 1976, the authority of the Lebanese state was briefly restored under the aegis of Syria. The first decree issued by the newly formed Lebanese government on 1 January 1977 imposed prior censorship on the press. Newspapers were examined before publication and censored passages filled before distribution to hide the blanks left by the censor. The procedure proved tedious and quickly fell into disuse. It was revived briefly under the Amin Gemayel government in 1982 after the Israeli invasion, but finally abrogated by Parliament in 1985.

In June 1977, in lieu of direct censorship, the government adopted Decree 104. This provided for such pre-judicial punishments as the precautionary detention of journalists and the administrative suspension of newspapers pending the verdict of the court. It also stiffened post-publication penalties for press offences: up to three-year prison terms for accused journalists and publishers and one-year closure of newspapers. A wide range of offences was defined by the law. These included 'defaming, libelling or insulting the president of the republic, or the head of state of a foreign government'. The public prosecutor was given the right to initiate prosecution in such cases without complaint from the aggrieved party. The immunity enjoyed by members of parliament was denied the press who could be prosecuted for publishing a statement by an MP deemed insulting to, or highly critical of, the president of the republic.

Lebanon at war: choose a side and stick to the story

Legal action was allowed against journalists and newspapers for publishing articles 'stirring sectarian animosities or endangering the security of the state'. Adopted at the behest of Syria and other Arab countries anxious to muzzle the Lebanese press, Decree 104 remained a dead letter in a state increasingly unable to assert its authority countrywide.

Growing financial problems added to the hardships of war. By the end of the war in 1990, the collapse of the Lebanese pound in 1982 together with increases in paper prices and the loss of advertising revenue to the 50 or so new, privately-owned TV stations had reduced most papers to a four-page format.

Nor did peace improve their situation. With the withdrawal of subsidies from their foreign Arab patrons, the press was forced to confront the law of the market where competition is keen and production costs high. Today, 10 dailies compete for a tiny readership. The total daily circulation of all newspapers is officially 70,000 though the figure is probably nearer 50,000. Newspapers are too expensive for most people and production costs preclude price cuts. A newspaper selling for LL1,000 does not cover costs estimated at LL1,500 (US$1) per copy.

Newspapers must also compete with television for viewers and advertising revenues. According to a poll published by *an-Nahar* (The Day) newspaper in 1991, while 86 per cent of Lebanese follow news on a regular basis, only 21 per cent do so through a newspaper; 40 per cent watch TV news; 30 per cent prefer radio. In 1993, only 20 per cent of Lebanon's advertising budget — US$152 million — was allocated to the daily press. Recent legislation reasserting state control over broadcasting, which should lead to the closure of most private television stations, could change this in its favour.

Their financial difficulties have made the press susceptible to financial inducement from politically ambitious businessmen. These include undeclared subsidies to newspapers and pay-offs to journalists. The personal media empire of Prime Minister Rafik Hariri includes a TV channel, a radio station and a 30 per cent holding in *an Nahar*, the most successful independent daily in Lebanon.

Some progress has been made in reversing repressive legislation. At the end of the war, the government revived the numerous press regulations, particularly Decree 104. From 1991, this has been used to harass the press, culminating in the 1993 prosecution of three opposition newspapers on various pretexts. In 1994, following protest by the press association backed by Parliament, the government was forced to abrogate two of its most pernicious provisions: the precautionary detention of journalists and the administrative suspension of newspapers in advance of a court verdict. The imprisonment of journalists and the closure of newspapers were, however, retained as legal punishments and the value of fines was raised.

But fear remains the greatest silencer. Self-censorship enables journalists to steer clear of a whole range of taboos more effectively than any law. No-one challenges Syria. Its *de facto* authority over Lebanon is complete and fear of treading on its sensibilities means that any useful discussion of Syrian domestic politics, Syria's role in Lebanon, Syrian-Israeli peace negotiations or the Lebanese armed resistance in south Lebanon is absent. The rare critical comment is couched in language so obscure as to be incomprehensible to the average reader.

The extension of press freedom is unlikely in the present political climate. Indeed, Syrian dominance in Lebanese affairs begs the question whether a free press is possible in a society that is itself not free. ❏

Carol Hakim, a member of St Antony's College, Oxford, was Beirut correspondent for Agence France Presse from 1980-1986

essential READING

—**INDEX** subscriber

United Kingdom & Overseas (excluding USA & Canada)

		UK:		Overseas:		Students: £25
1 year—6 issues		£36		£42		
2 years—12 issues		£65		£77		
3 years—18 issues		£95		£113		

Name

Address

Postcode   B6A2

£ _____ total. ❏ Cheque (£) ❏ Visa/Mastercard ❏ Am Ex ❏ Diners Club

Card No.

Expiry   Signature

❏ I would also like to send **INDEX** to a reader in the developing world—just £23. These sponsored subscriptions promote free speech around the world for only the cost of printing and postage.

❏ I do not wish to receive mail from other companies.

INDEX, Freepost, 33 Islington High Street, London N1 9BR **Telephone:** 0171 278 2313

United States and Canada

		US:	Students:
1 year—6 issues		$50	$35
2 years—12 issues		$92	
3 years—18 issues		$130	

Name

Address

Postcode   B6B2

$ _____ total. ❏ Check (US$) ❏ Visa/Mastercard ❏ Am Ex ❏ Diners Club

Card No.

Expiry   Signature

❏ I would also like to send **INDEX** to a reader in the developing world—just £23. These sponsored subscriptions promote free speech around the world for only the cost of printing and postage.

❏ I do not wish to receive mail from other companies.

INDEX

33 Islington High Street, London N1 9LH England Facsimile: 0171 278 1878
Email: indexoncenso@gn.apc.org   http://www.oneworld.org/index_oc/

INDEX ON CENSORSHIP
33 Islington High Street
London N1 9BR
United Kingdom

BUSINESS REPLY MAIL

FIRST CLASS PERMIT NO.7796 NEW YORK, NY

Postage will be paid by addressee.

INDEX ON CENSORSHIP
215 Park Avenue South
11th Floor
New York, NY 10211-0997

MICHAL SELA & IAN BLACK

Editorial and military censors

Concentration of ownership is the main threat to Israel's once vibrant and combative press

Rome 1986: the muzzling of Mordechai Vanunu

ISRAEL is unique in the Middle East both for the dynamism of its democratic political institutions and its news-addicted society. This is reflected in a press which many Israelis believe is too critical for its own good. The Israeli print media is like the Israelis themselves: noisy, brash, argumentative and very self-obsessed.

Yet behind this appearance of a free press, oppression comes in three distinct forms. As in many western states, the Israeli press suffers from the economic pressures of concentration. A handful of papers dominate the market and drive out alternative perspectives. The intensity of competition has driven the market leaders *Yedioth Ahronoth* (Latest News) and *Ma'ariv* (Evening Prayer) to the absurd lengths of wiretapping each others' editorial offices, a saga which has preoccupied the Israeli courts for two years and led to the resignation of *Yedioth's* editor, Moshe Vardi, in February 1996. His rival, Ofer Nimrodi, is currently on trial facing the same charge. Yet the scandals have only helped preserve the two papers' market shares, which slowly drives other papers out of business. Even such an established paper as the Histadrut labour federation's 71-year-old daily *Davar* (The Word) has been driven to the brink of closure. The Histadrut announced the last issue of *Davar* would be printed on 16 February 1996. On the eve of closure, the Barnea-Zinger group emerged with a bid backed by 30 industrial concerns to bail out the paper on 15 February. Under its new name, *Davar Rishon* will have two years to establish its niche or face closure.

More particular to Israel are the press laws and their enforcer, the military censor. Israel's press laws are a draconian inheritance from the British Mandate. The first dates back to the press ordinance of 1933 and entrusts the minister of the interior with the authority to issue newspaper licences, establish the competence of editors and close any newspaper deemed a threat to public order, without judicial review. It has seldom affected the mainstream Hebrew-language press, though in the mid-1980s the now-defunct tabloid *Hadashot* was closed down for some days for a breach of censorship when it reported on the cover-up of secret service killings of Palestinian prisoners. More commonly, the ordinance has been applied against the radical fringe of Israeli papers and all Palestinian newspapers published in East Jerusalem under Israeli law.

The second law derived from emergency regulations and established the military censor. In effect, the law requires that all news items that concern the security of the state and public order be subject to the approval of the military censor. State security and public order can receive the widest possible interpretation: names of soldiers killed in operations cannot be published until officially released by the military in the interest of public morale; the name of the director of the Shin Bet secret service cannot be published — though his identity is practically a household name in Israel. Correspondents who fail to respect these restrictions find themselves summoned to the Censor's Office where they are grilled by an officer with a copy of the offending article marked up in red ink.

While every correspondent has anecdotes of brushes with the awful Colonel Avi — one recent incumbent in the Censor's Office in Jerusalem — it is clear that the government is losing its ability to contain the flow of information. In some instances, Israeli journalists simply brave the censor by publishing regardless of restrictions. More commonly, they leak stories to foreign correspondents which, once published abroad, can be freely reported in Israel citing the foreign newspaper.

Faced with the absurdity of containing common knowledge, the military censor tends to overlook many infractions, as in the challenges posed to the ban on publishing the name of the director of the Shin Bet security service. It was considered an act of daring when one newspaper made a pun of outgoing head of Shin Bet Yakov Peri's name in an article purporting to be about TV lawyer Perry Mason. Peri's name appeared in the headline quite unmistakably to anyone who bothered to read it. The military censor conceded the right to refer to Peri's successor Karmi Gilon by his first initial — Kaf. Upon his resignation in January 1996, in the wake of Prime Minister Rabin's assassination, the state television broadcast a biography of the man they still referred to simply as Kaf. It was only when *Ha'aretz* (The Land) defied the censors by publishing the name of Kaf's successor, Ami Ayalon, that the veil of secrecy was lifted and, citing an article in the *Washington Post*, Kaf's full name passed from street graffiti to newsprint. In a series of editorials the press now calls for changes to secrecy laws. The Ministries of Justice and of the Interior have responded to journalists' demands by convening a special review panel

BIR ZEIT AND HEBRON UNIVERSITIES "PALESTINE WEEK"

The one they didn't print: cartoon banned by the Israeli censor

to examine the press laws, which first met on 22 February 1996. The panel, which is composed of journalists, jurists and academics, has a broad mandate to make recommendations and is perceived as sympathetic to press freedoms. It is expected to produce proposals for revising the press laws, though it has not been empowered to draft a new law. Yet many journalists see the drafting of a new law as a logical outcome of the process.

Particular to Israel is the collusion between newspaper editors and the government censors known as the 'Editors' Committee'. This voluntary club of editors has an agreement with the military censor and the government to be briefed periodically about things they agree not to

publish. Playing on a journalist's vanity to be in the know, the restrictions against publishing information thus obtained compromise the integrity of the press. When the military censor and the prime minister asked editors not to report on the Egyptian troop build-up along the Suez Canal in October 1973 so as not to provoke a panic among the public, many later regretted their part in the national unpreparedness revealed in the early days of the Yom Kippur War. The Editors' Committee can also be counter-productive. In 1986, Mordechai Vanunu provided details on Israel's nuclear weapons programme to *The Sunday Times* in London. The paper suspected Vanunu of fraud until information was leaked from the Editors' Committee that the Israeli press was not to publish a thing on the story. That was confirmation enough for *The Sunday Times* who ran the story on 5 October. Once it was out and government censorship bypassed, the Israeli press was free to publish Vanunu's account.

These instruments of self-censorship have come under sustained attack from the press, led by the liberal daily *Ha'aretz*. Editor-in-chief Marmari Chanoch first challenged the 1966 Censorship Agreement, which established an arbitration procedure between the Editors' Committee and the military censor. While continuing to respect the law and submit material to the military censor, Chanoch announced that his paper would, as of November 1992, take future disputes over censorship to the Israeli courts rather than the arbitration mechanism. In September 1995 Chanoch challenged outright the need for the Editors' Committee. In a stormy meeting of the committee he proposed the group disband and publish a joint statement reaffirming their commitment to an independent and critical press. The measure was voted down, and on 20 September Chanoch wrote to the secretary of the committee to announce *Ha'aretz*'s unilateral withdrawal. The market-leading tabloid *Yedioth Ahronoth* followed suit soon after. These defections have rendered the Editors' Committee a dead letter.

Vestiges of official censorship for strictly security reasons seem likely to remain, but as the role of the military in society becomes less important and there is less obeisance to once sacred cows, the Israeli press will become more 'normal' — for better and for worse. ❏

Michal Sela is a correspondent on Palestinian affairs with the Israeli daily Davar
Ian Black was the Jerusalem correspondent and is now diplomatic editor of the British daily Guardian

KHALIL ABU ARAFEH

Cartoon crossfire

I HAVE a hard time as a cartoonist: I face censorship directly from the Israeli military and indirectly from the Palestinian National Authority. In my experience the Israeli censor will not approve cartoons about Israeli soldiers, settlers, fanatic Jews, or anything that might be construed as incitement against Israel or Israel's occupation. As to the PNA, my cartoons are not allowed to criticise it or its policy at all. I'm not allowed to draw Arafat or any member of the PNA. They consider these drawings an insult. But I don't believe that cheering the Authority is my job. I am going to go on working and criticising albeit in a symbolic, and maybe subtle, way.

Me and my problems: Khalil Abu Arafeh

PRISONERS OF WAR IN ISRAEL

RUBA HUSSARI

Arafat's law

Since Arafat's return to Gaza and Jericho in May 1994, arrests of journalists, detention without trial, and the closures of newspapers have created an atmosphere of fear in which self-censorship and silence flourish

FORMAL press controls were given legal sanction in the July 1995 press law introduced by executive fiat when Arafat was the sole legislative authority. The political motives behind this became apparent in the electoral campaign for the presidency and legislative council in January 1996. In the aftermath of the polls, the prospects for freedom of expression look grim so long as the shaping of the institutions of self-rule remain under Arafat's law.

Professional journalism is a relative novelty in the Palestinian territories of the West Bank and Gaza Strip. Before the intifada, the press was a political tool dedicated to communicating information from the exiled Palestinian Liberation Organisation (PLO) leadership in Beirut and later Tunis, and to promoting the struggle against Israeli occupation. The first newspaper to open following the Israeli occupation in 1967 was *al-Quds* (Jerusalem). Owned by Marwan Abu Zuluf in partnership with a Jordanian newspaper, it suffered from its association with Jordan and its pro-Hashemite line. Today, a much changed *al-Quds* is the largest Arabic daily in Jerusalem. In 1972, Palestinian–American Paul Ajluni opened the daily *al-Fajr* (The Dawn) and Mahmud Yaish began to publish *al-Sha'ab* (The People), both with the financial support of the PLO.

These three papers constituted the 'national press' of Palestinians under Israeli occupation and, like the trade unions, women's charitable organisations, or the research institutes, were seen as national institutions. Financed by the PLO, they recruited for the PLO and provided jobs for

PLO veterans. Retired ideologues from the PLO wrote newspaper articles in lieu of political tracts. They were journalists with no knowledge of the basics. Given their role in engaging the struggle against occupation through the office of the military censor, the public forgave the papers their mistakes.

Of all the Occupied Territories, only East Jerusalem came under Israeli law following its annexation in 1967. Palestinians thus enjoyed the legal right to publish newspapers in Jerusalem, though Israeli law provided ample means of censorship through emergency regulations inherited from the British Mandate. The man in uniform sitting in Israel's Government Press Office's first floor was the real editor of the newspapers. He exercised comprehensive prior censorship on every section of a paper — features, editorials, cartoons, photographs, advertisements, even obituaries. As newsrooms attempted to second-guess the censor, self-styled journalists who knew nothing of the basic skills of the trade, resorted to self-censorship and subterfuge. The consequence was an amateur press.

The intifada marked a point of departure. The role of public mobilisation passed from the national papers, which came under yet more stringent censorship, to the leaflets circulated by the underground command of the uprising. In the aftermath of the Gulf War, when the PLO was cut off at the pockets by Saudi Arabia and Kuwait for its support of Saddam Hussein, *al-Fajr* and *al-Sha'ab* disappeared, unremarked, from the newsstands in 1993. They had become irrelevant.

The amateur journalists of the national press were replaced by new professionals bred by the intifada. Foreign

KHALIL ABU ARAFEH

What Arafat didn't want to see

journalists in pursuit of the intifada flooded the Occupied Territories and hired local journalists who worked alongside them. Freed for the first time from the demands of propaganda, Palestinian journalists developed into independent professionals able to steal the scene from political activists.

This development was not welcomed by Arafat. Two months after his return in May 1994, he banned the distribution of the East Jerusalem daily an-Nahar (The Day) in the West Bank and Gaza Strip. Cut off from their markets, the newspaper's editors were forced to suspend publication. Founded in 1986, the paper followed a pro-Jordanian line and, with King Hussein signing independent peace agreements with Israel, Arafat's banning was a means of communicating his own message to Jordan: don't attempt to extend your influence into my territory. A Palestinian security agent interviewed by Israeli broadcasters confirmed that the Palestinian National Authority (PNA) would not tolerate any newspaper loyal to another state publishing in its territory. A very cautious an-Nahar reappeared a few weeks later after an understanding was reached between Arafat and the paper's publisher and editor.

Two new opposition newspapers were licensed in Gaza: al-Watan (The Nation) supported by the Islamic opposition movement Hamas, and al-Istiqlal (The Independent) associated with the harder-line Islamic Jihad. It was but a matter of months before Arafat came into confrontation with the two papers, both highly critical of his negotiations with Israel. Early in 1995, seven journalists from al-Istiqlal were arrested by Palestinian police. They were not officially charged and were not allowed lawyers. All were released after periods of detention ranging from a few weeks to a few months. Al-Watan was next: its staff were detained for varying periods and its editor, Sayyid Abu Musameh, sentenced by the newly-created security courts to three years' imprisonment for incitement. The paper's successive closures and reappearances reflect the state of dialogue between Arafat and Hamas.

The Publications and Publishing Law of 1995, a 51-article document signed by Arafat in his dual capacities as president of the Executive Council of the PLO and president of the PNA on 25 June 1995, formalised relations between the PNA and the press. The law sets out the legal procedures to be observed against offending publications. Yet since its introduction, both al-Watan and al-Istiqlal have faced closure (August 1995) and journalists have been arrested (three reporters with an-Nahar were detained without charge in Gaza on 30 August) without formal charges or the issuing of warrants. By the end of September 1995, Reporters sans Frontières (RSF) had lodged more than 20 protests with the Palestinian authorities on the detention and ill-treatment of journalists, the seizure of newspapers, and the closure of newspaper offices. It called for a review of the press law and curbs on security forces.

With the January elections looming, all Arafat wanted from the press was top billing in their pages. To a great extent, the intimidated press complied. But when *al-Quds'* night editor Maher al-Alami made the grave mistake of burying on page eight the compliment from the Greek Orthodox Patriarch likening Arafat to the seventh-century Arab caliph Umar, who delivered Jerusalem to Islam, instead of featuring it on page one with a banner headline, he was summoned to Jericho by security forces on Christmas Eve, detained for six days and released after a personal reprimand from Arafat.

Inherent in the new Palestinian electoral law is the principle of equal access to the official news and current affairs media. This principle was overlooked in the interest of the PLO's electoral success. RSF claimed that between 15-25 December Arafat enjoyed over one hour of Palestinian TV airtime, while his rival Samiha Khalil received none; and that Arafat's Fatah candidates enjoyed 71 minutes of airtime compared to 17 seconds for the Palestine People's Party. The 19 other parties contesting the election had no airtime.

The sizeable block of opposition candidates who won seats in the Legislative Council reflected the appeal of individuals who promised to act as a check on Arafat's authority, such as Haydar Abdel Shafi in Gaza or Hanan Ashrawi in Jerusalem rather than any critical role played by the press. RSF election monitors claimed that journalists worked in 'a climate of intimidation and fear obvious in the way the public media and the press covered the elections'. Former US president Jimmy Carter also accused the Arafat government: 'There's not an adequate commitment to freedom of the press and criticism of the Authority has not been permitted.'

None of which is unusual in the history of state-formation in the Middle East, but it is unfortunate that on the eve of the 21st century, instead of creating a national press that reflects its time, the PNA are moving back to square one. ❏

Ruba Hussari *is Jerusalem correspondent for the London-based Arabic daily* al-Hayat *and a reporter for BBC Arabic service radio and television*

ISMET IMSET

Turkish roulette

The freedom enjoyed by Turkey's profuse and colourful daily newspapers does not extend to their Kurdish counterparts

For the most part, the press in Turkey is free of pre-publication censorship. The leading dailies publish more or less without government impediment and enjoy wide circulations. In spring 1994 these ranged between 60,000 copies for the leftist-nationalist *Cumhuriyet* (The Republic), to 300,000 for the Islamist *Türkiye*; secular rivals *Hürriyet* (Freedom) and *Milliyet* (Nation) sold between 450-650,000; 700,000 for market leader *Sabah* (Morning).

The same rules did not apply to one particular daily with distribution figures at the low end of the scale (50,000). *Özgür Gündem* (Free Agenda) was considered subversive and closed down in 1994. Subversive newspapers are legal and allowed to publish under Turkish law. They also pay taxes. However, they are subject to various forms of official censorship, such as confiscation and closure orders issued by state prosecutors. They are also subject to a wide range of unofficial measures. Targets since the 1970s include Communist and other leftist publications. But since 1984 it is dominantly the pro-Kurdish press that has been deemed subversive (see *Index* Turkey File 1/1995).

On 30 November 1994, Prime Minister Tansu Çiller issued a secret decree to various government offices (later leaked to the press) urging action for 'the elimination of all dangerous media' in the country. By 'dangerous' she meant the dissident and left-wing media critical of Ankara's refusal to give Turkey's ethnic Kurds social or cultural rights. The primary target of the decree had already been identified days before in a military-dominated National Security Council meeting as *Özgür Ülke* (Free Country), successor to the closed *Özgür Gündem*.

In the early hours of 3 December, the four-storey printing facility of

Cizre, southeast Turkey 1995: portrait of a dead guerrilla

Özgür Ülke in Istanbul was hit by a bomb which, in the words of its editor-in-chief Baki Karadeniz, left the building 'as if struck by an air raid'. The daily's editorial headquarters were simultaneously destroyed by a second bomb. In a third explosion some 200 miles away, *Özgür Ülke*'s central office in Ankara was blown up. One newspaper worker was killed and 18 others injured.

In response to foreign pressure, Ankara made a face-saving gesture and announced that the paper would be compensated for its damages — a promise the government has yet to honour. Instead, new court cases and investigations were launched against *Özgür Ülke* and more and more journalists faced arbitrary detentions. With international interest in the matter declining, in January 1995 the authorities changed tactics against the paper. In a subsequent meeting of the National Security Council, the decision was taken to eliminate 'all of the dissident press in Turkey...within the limits of the law'.

Özgür Ülke *1995: the mark of the beast*

Beginning on 6 January, policemen took up position outside the printing facilities of *Özgür Ülke* to confiscate the paper as it was printed. With newspaper coverage of human rights issues running up to three or four pages per issue, all undesirable items were censored and the paper forced to reprint. In the second week of the campaign the reprinted newspapers began to appear with the mark 'censored' in lieu of stories. Even stories that appeared completely uncensored in the mass dailies were censored in the pro-Kurdish press. *Özgür Ülke* was allowed to publish less and less on human rights and the Kurdish issue. By the third week of January the paper had to publish two to three times a day to avoid confiscation. Turkey's mainstream journalists watched without intervening.

Outside Istanbul, a more violent campaign was taking place against the newspaper. In the eastern Anatolian city of Diyarbakir the paper's office was raided by the police. At least five reporters were detained and extensively tortured. Staff members in Turkey and abroad received threats.

As the ruthless campaign continued, the Press Council chairman Oktay Eksi made a public appeal for a conclusion of the campaign. Writing in his column in *Hürriyet*, a paper that had campaigned systematically against *Özgür Ülke*, Eksi had his way. In February a Magistrates Court judge ordered the confiscation of all copies of the paper. When it continued to print, another judge passed an order for its closure. Legally, *Özgür Ülke* could no longer publish. In all, more than 230 published issues had been seized. The cost in human terms was even higher.

A total of 23 journalists have been assassinated for writing for the two papers, *Özgür Gündem* and *Özgür Ülke*. Four reporters have disappeared and only one tortured body, that of a reporter kidnapped by police, has been found. By the end of 1995, 35 employees were still serving prison terms, including every editor of the paper. The former owner of the newspaper, Yaşar Kaya, faces 1,200 years imprisonment for publication crimes.

At the end of 1995, in a final attempt to satisfy European critics, Turkey amended its controversial Article 8 of the anti-terrorism law under which most of the above had been charged, and opened the doors to the promised customs union with Europe. Turkish officials promised Europe they would take immediate steps to restore human rights and freedom of expression. Since then, arrests and detentions of journalists as well as heavy censorship of the printed and television media have been continuing at the same pace, signalling no change despite the release of a token number of 'selected' criminals of thought.

In January 1996, for instance, Metin Göktepe, a journalist with the leftist Istanbul-based daily *Evrensel*, was detained by police while covering the funeral of two leftist militants killed in a prison clash. His lifeless body, with a cracked skull, was found dumped in a park the next day. The risks for those who would write for the 'subversive press' in Turkey are undiminished. ❏

Ismet Imset *was a journalist for the English-language* Turkish Daily News *and for the pro-Kurdish paper* Özgür Gündem. *He is now based in London*

These essays are based on lectures presented at the Middle East Centre, St Antony's College, Oxford in the autumn term of 1995. I am grateful to Saïd Essoulami of Article 19 and Trevor Mostyn of MED-MEDIA for their participation, and to the Near Eastern Studies Programme at Oxford for its financial support **ER**

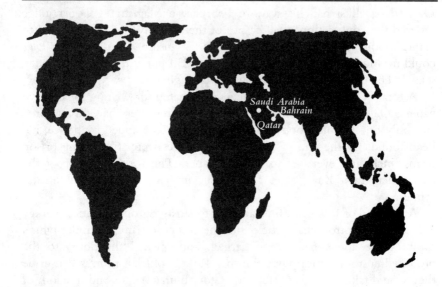

A little local difficulty

It's been a busy couple of months in Bahrain: demonstrations, mass arrests, torture, forced deportations, and all the rest. Why do the disturbances in this tiny and not very populous island in the Gulf matter? Apart from the fact that people are being beaten up, rounded up and locked up for voicing their (mostly peaceful) opposition to the Emir's autocratic rule, the ripples have spread far beyond the villages around Manama.

Fifteen months of unrest there have shed a rare light on the practice of politics among the member states of the Gulf Co-operation Council, which comprises some of the most inscrutably anti-democratic regimes on the planet. With democracy threatening to break out in Bahrain, and with Qatar ploughing an increasingly independent furrow, the other GCC states are worried that the regional stability on which trade ties with the West are built, and which rests on a ruthless stifling of dissent, is in danger of fracture.

Then, at the start of February, eight prominent Kuwaiti MPs (Kuwait is the only Gulf state to have elected MPs, in a Parliament disbanded in 1986 and reconvened after the Gulf War) wrote to the Emir of Bahrain asking him to give serious consideration to the demonstrators' demands: the restoration of Parliament and the constitution, which he dissolved in 1975. Coming from a close ally, such 'friendly fire' was hardly welcome.

'It's a human rights issue that we have addressed,' said one of the signatories to the letter. 'It shouldn't cause sensitivities. Human rights issues are international and unlimited.' The Emir doesn't see things that way. His government prefers to put out the story that all the demonstrations are caused by a few troublemakers among the 60 per cent Shia population, inspired and manipulated by Iran, which is bent on extending its power in the region. The roots of the trouble are not religious: this convenient construct, guaranteed to alert the sympathies of the Emir's western allies, masks enormous social and political dissatisfaction across the country.

If there is any hidden hand in this complex shadowplay, it belongs to the all-powerful House of Saud, the prime mover behind the GCC. An attempted coup in Qatar on 19 February, to bring back the Emir ousted by his more intractable son last summer, is strongly suspected to have been given the nod from Riyadh, with support from neighbouring Bahrain, with whom Qatar has a long-standing border dispute.

As the case of Mohammed al-Mas'ari shows, Saudi Arabia is quite adept at bending other countries to its will. There are reports that Bahrain has also tried to exert pressure on the British government to take similar action against émigré activists in London. This is not surprising since large revenues from oil and arms contracts depend on preserving the facade that all is well in the Gulf, apart from a little local difficulty.

But lies often have a price, and this time it is being paid on the streets of Manama. The West, through its defence ministries, oil conglomerates and munitions industries, sees an unambiguous interest in making sure Bahrain succeeds in quashing the unrest. They do not seem to have learned the lesson from the Iranian revolution 17 years ago, that propping up despots in difficulties can be more costly in the end. At the moment, if they have any interest in democracy, it is tangential at best. As long as the business climate in the Gulf is favourable, they will go on doing business. And the Gulf's would-be democrats can be damned. ❑

Adam Newey

A censorship chronicle incorporating information from Agence France-Presse (AFP), the American Association for the Advancement of Science Human Rights Action Network (AAASHRAN), Amnesty International (AI), Article 19 (A19), the BBC Monitoring Service Summary of World Broadcasts (SWB), the Committee to Protect Journalists (CPJ), the Canadian Committee to Protect Journalists (CCPJ), the Inter-American Press Association (IAPA), the International Federation of Journalists (IFJ/FIP), the International Federation of Newspaper Publishers (FIEJ), Human Rights Watch (HRW), the Media Institute of Southern Africa (MISA), International PEN (PEN), Open Media Research Institute Daily Digest (OMRI), Reporters Sans Frontières (RSF) and other sources.

ALBANIA

It was reported in December that the Socialist Party has decided not to put forward a number of prominent members as candidates in the forthcoming elections, including party general secretary Gramoz Ruci. Under the Genocide Law, many people who held public office before 1991 are barred from standing for Parliament (*Index* 6/1995). In January the Constitutional Court rejected as 'groundless' appeals against the Genocide Law and the Verification Law, which allows selective access to former secret police files (*Index* 1/1996). (OMRI)

On 26 January police seized six delivery trucks belonging to

Koha Jone, preventing the distribution of the daily and 11 other independent opposition papers. Although the 37,000 copies of *Koha Jone* were returned, the trucks remained in police hands. (RSF)

On 31 January *Koha Jone* journalist Altin Hazizaj was detained for three days and charged with assaulting two police officers while reporting the eviction of former political prisoners from illegally occupied apartments in Tirana. Genc Shkullaku, a photographer for the paper, had his camera confiscated while covering the same event. It was initially reported that the charges against Hazizaj had been dropped but it now appears that the matter is still under investigation. He denies assaulting the two officers. (HRW)

Recent publication: *Press Restrictions in Albania* (Minnesota Advocates for Human Rights, December 1995, 45pp)

ALGERIA

Outoudert Abrous, editor-in-chief of daily *Liberté*, and Hacene Ouandjli, the paper's editor, were arrested on 10 December and the newspaper suspended for 15 days by the Ministry of the Interior following the publication on 7 December of an article about General Betchine, an adviser to President Zeroual, which the ministry claimed was inaccurate. Independent newspapers went on strike for three days in protest. Ouandjli was released on 12 December but Abrous and *Liberté*

journalist Samir Kmayaz received suspended sentences for publishing false information. Nine journalists resigned from the daily *L'Authentique* following their newspaper's criticism of the strike. (RSF, Reuter)

Mohamed Belkacem, who worked for state-run television ENTV, was kidnapped and murdered near his home in Baraki, southern Algiers, on 20 December. Mohamed Mekati, journalist with the government daily *El Moudjahid*, died of his wounds on 10 January after being shot near his home the day before by unidentified gunmen. Khaled Aboulkacem, archivist at *L'Indépendant* newspaper, was killed and Nourredine Guittoune, the paper's owner and editor-in-chief, was wounded in a gun attack as they left their offices on 13 January. And on 10 February Abdallah Bouhachek, editor of *Révolution et Travaille*, the UGTA workers' union paper, was shot dead while on his way to work near Blida. (CPJ, *Independent*)

On 10 February the Interior Ministry ordered newspaper editors to submit all reports of the ongoing civil war to a government censor before publication, on the grounds that coverage of civilian deaths undermines the security forces' campaign against Islamist guerrillas. More than 50,000 people have been killed since the cancellation of the 1992 elections, which precipitated the war. (RSF)

A car bomb exploded on 11 February outside the Tahar Djaout press centre in Algiers, killing 18 people and injuring over 50. Three journalists from the daily *Le Soir d'Algerie* — editor-in-chief Allaoua Ait M'barak, columnist Mohamed Dorbane, and staff writer Djamel Derraz — were among the dead. The centre houses several newspapers, including *Le Matin*, *L'Opinion* and *El Watan*, the offices of which were damaged in the attack. (CPJ)

ANGOLA

Journalist Alderto Costa of the government-owned *Radio Luanda* died after being shot five times at his home on the night of 19 December. The motive for the murder is unclear, but journalists are increasingly being targeted by political and criminal factions as they cover the escalating crime wave. (MISA)

A year on from the 18 January 1995 assassination of Ricardo de Mello, director of the independent *Imparcial Fax* (*Index* 2/1995), his case remains unsolved and threats and harassment against Angolan journalists continue. Several other *Imparcial Fax* editors have been forced into exile, while other journalists and editors are increasingly resorting to self-censorship. (RSF)

AUSTRALIA

In January five works by the Aboriginal artist Ray Thomas, commissioned by Melbourne City Council to mark sites of Aboriginal cultural importance, were withdrawn for being 'too confrontational'. One piece, depicting the head of an Aborigine impaled on the sword of justice, which was to go on display outside the Supreme Court, was vetoed after a complaint from Victoria's chief justice. (Melbourne *Age*)

The Internet free speech group Electronic Frontiers Australia made a submission to the federal inquiry into online services in mid-February, strongly criticising proposals to extend the Australian Broadcasting Authority's regulatory role over broadcast media to electronic communications (see http://www.iinet.au/griffin). (*Australian Financial Review*)

AZERBAIJAN

The first issue of 1996 of the opposition newspaper *Azadlyg* was banned by the censors because it contained an article criticising the amnesty announced by President Heydar Aliyev on 27 December, following the adoption of the new constitution. The article's author, Halig Bahadir, wrote that the amnesty is being applied only 'to those who do not criticise the current administration of the country and who are not dangerous for official Baku'. (SWB)

On 11 January Turan news agency announced that all media in the country must re-register with the Ministry of Press and Information between 12 and 30 January, or be banned. Azerbaijan radio reported that the media have been ordered to re-register because they are 'rampantly exploiting the principles of freedom of the press and information'. That is why a number of publications have not appeared for some time, the station said. (SWB)

Recent publication: *Allegations of Ill-Treatment in Detention* (AI, January 1996, 7pp)

BAHRAIN

On 19 December Ahmad al-Shamlan, a lawyer and writer, and Hafedh al-Sheikh, a journalist, were summoned to the Intelligence Department where they were threatened and ordered not to leave the country on account of a programme broadcast by Qatar Radio on 7 December in which they had called for democracy in Bahrain. On 20 December both men were charged with 'inciting hatred against the political system' and released on bail of US$1,500. On 20 December Sheikh Hassan Sultan was detained for preaching in favour of democracy. He was released after paying a fine of US$1,500. (Bahrain Human Rights Organisation)

On 22 January eight Shi'ite Muslim clerics, including Sheikh Abd al-Amir al-Jamri, a former member of parliament and pro-democracy activist (*Index* 3/1995, 4/1995, 6/1995), were arrested and charged with incitement and involvement in anti-government protests. Since the beginning of 1996 many mosques had been closed down or attacked by the police searching for 'subversive literature'. Hundreds of people have been arbitrarily detained, mostly for participation in peaceful gatherings calling for the release of political prisoners, restoration of the dissolved Parliament and reactivation of the suspended constitution. (Bahrain Human Rights Organisation, Reuter)

On 7 February Ahmad al-Shamlan (see above) was again detained by members of the Intelligence Department. Al-Shamlan had been invited to give a talk on democracy at the Al-Oroobah Club on 6 February, but the department intervened and cancelled the meeting. He has apparently been accused of playing an 'active role' in recent acts of arson and sabotage, and of involvement with 'suspicious foreign organisations', presumably referring to Iran. On 3 February the Committee for Popular Petition (CPP), of which al-Shamlan is a member, distributed a statement condemning the Arabic-language media for deliberately falsifying news and accusing the jailed pro-democracy activists of linkage with foreign powers. (Bahrain Freedom Movement, Reuter, PEN)

BELARUS

On 4 January President Lukasenka issued a decree 'On certain issues of state information policy'. Among other things, it states that 'the chief editors of national periodical publications financed from the national budget [which means almost all main periodicals], with the exception of the newspapers *Zviazda*, *Sovetskaya Belorussiya*, and *Narodnaya Hazieta* and the magazine *Belaruskaya Dumka*

shall be appointed by the Cabinet of Ministers after consultation with the Presidential Administration'; that 'town and district publishing houses are to be handed over to the executive committees of local bodies of power'; that 'state-run national and local periodical publications shall receive specific supplies of paper from the State Committee for the Press'; and that 'graduates of the journalism faculty of the Belarusian State University shall be assigned to work in district and town newspapers.' (SWB)

Lithuanian radio reported on 14 January that since the beginning of the year the Belarusian opposition paper *Svaboda* (*Index* 1/1995, 5/1995) has been printed in Vilnius by *Lietuvos Rytas*, Lithuania's largest daily paper, after a printing works in Orsa was forbidden to extend its contract by Vladimir Zametalin, head of the Presidential administration. *Svaboda* is the fifth Belarusian paper to have to print in Vilnius. (SWB)

BOLIVIA

On 20 December, 170 peasant women from coca-growing communities were arrested while marching from Cochabamba to La Paz to seek a dialogue with the government about its coca-eradication programme as well as about human rights abuses that have taken place in the course of it. The government had previously announced that it would allow the march to go ahead. The women were

released during the following two days. A further 48 women and children were detained on 27 December during another march. (AI)

BOSNIA-HERCEGOVINA

On 7 February *Nasa Borba* reported that Bosnian Serb authorities in Pale prevented the mayor of Banja Luka, Pedrag Radic, from meeting US president Bill Clinton's special envoy, Robert Galucci. (OMRI)

On 8 February Bosnian Serb police in Sarajevo detained two Associated Press photographers near a bridge connecting Serb and government-held parts. Srdjan Ilic, who is based in Belgrade, was released the next day but Hidajet Delic, who also works for BH Press, the Bosnian government news agency, is still in detention, probably in Pale. (CPJ)

BULGARIA

On 12 December the Constitutional Court overruled Parliament's decision to transfer some of its legal powers to the parliamentary commission for radio, TV and the state news agency. Parliament's decision followed a previous court ruling declaring the 'provisional statute' on the media unconstitutional (*Index* 6/1995). The court also ruled that the commission may not decide on the management of state media, structural changes, programme schedules or the media's statutes. The commission may still nominate directors of state media and propose legislation on media issues. The decision followed one week after an interview with President Zhelyu Zhelev in the daily *Trud*, in which he warned that attempts by the Bulgarian Socialist Party parliamentary majority to 'control and directly guide radio and television programmes' constitute a grave danger to freedom of expression. (OMRI, SWB)

Seven journalists were dismissed from Bulgarian national radio on 18 December after they protested against censorship in the national press. The opposition Union of Democratic Forces called for their reinstatement and the immediate resignation of Vyacheslav Tunev, head of Bulgarian National Radio. Next day President Zhelev, at an impromptu news conference in Lisbon, said 'Two days ago, Bulgaria submitted its official application for EU membership. However, I find it difficult to believe that anyone will talk to us seriously if a national medium such as Bulgarian radio dismisses leading journalists in such a brutal manner. Everyone should react against this act... It confirms that the national media are turning into uniquely party institutions that are commanded directly by the party headquarters of the ruling majority.' (SWB)

BURMA

On 16 December U Sein Hla Aung was arrested for distributing videos of Aung San Suu Kyi's 'People's Forum', the informal gatherings which have taken place outside her home since her release from house arrest in July 1995. (HRW)

Thirteen performance artists were detained in Mandalay between 7 and 10 January. Of the 13, nine are members of the *A Nyein* song and dance troupe, and two are comedians who had participated in a private Independence Day celebration at the home of Aung San Suu Kyi on 4 January. The leader of the troupe, U Pa Pa Lay, was previously arrested in 1991, and served a two-year prison sentence for his satire of the military government. (HRW)

Imprisoned journalists Myo Myint Nyein, editor-in-chief of the cultural magazine *What's Happening* and Win Tin, former editor of the newspaper *Hanthawati*, have reportedly been severely ill-treated in prison. Conditions include being forced to sleep in solitary confinement on concrete floors without mats or blankets, in cells where military dogs are usually kept. Khin Zaw Win, sentenced to 15 years in 1994 (*Index* 4/1994, 6/1994), has been reported to be suffering similar treatment. (AAASHRAN, RSF)

BURUNDI

On 13 January Jean Hélène, East Africa correspondent for *Le Monde* and Radio France Internationale, was permitted to leave Burundi after being being prevented from doing so by the police. He was arrested on 10 January and released after an hour, but prevented from taking his flight the next day. He attributes the incident to his reports on the problems of Hutus now living under Tutsi rule. He was formerly prevented from returning to Rwanda owing to his reporting on the genocide of the Tutsis by the Hutus. (CPJ)

The genocide in Burundi continues to gain momentum. In a letter to the UN Security Council released on 3 January, UN secretary-general Boutros Boutros Ghali warned that the violence could '...explode on a massive scale' and called for the preparation of a military force that could intervene. The Security Council does not favour this approach. The situation continued to deteriorate throughout the month of January with the assassination of prominent politician Bede Nzobonimpa, governor of the northern province of Ngozi, on 22 January and a grenade assault on four relief groups in the capital of Bujumbura on 24 January. A recent UN report put the civilian death toll at 200 a week. (*Guardian*, *International Herald Tribune*, *Independent*)

CAMBODIA

Ek Mongkol, a well-known announcer for the station Radio 90, was shot and seriously wounded in the neck and chest as he left the station's Phnom Penh offices on 8 February. The attack, by four men in civilian clothing, is believed to be related to comments Ek Mongkol had made about an alleged Vietnamese offensive in eastern Cambodia. (RSF)

Preliminary court hearings began against the newspaper *Neak Proyuth* (The Combatant) on 8 February. The paper, which is linked to the opposition Khmer Nation Party (KNP) is charged with libel and disturbing the public order in connection with a series of articles published in January criticising the 'exclusive power' of the government. (RSF)

CANADA

The government is moving to impose strict measures to ban virtually all cigarette advertising, sponsorship and corporate promotion, despite the September 1995 ruling of the Supreme Court that the 1988 Tobacco Products Control Act is an unconstitutional infringement of free speech rights (*Index* 6/1995). The new measures go well beyond the act. (*International Herald Tribune*)

Keith Spicer, CRTC chairman, has backed down on threats to ban any violent US programming (*Index* 1/1996). Spicer wanted to put pressure on the US to develop a rating sytem to rate programmes according to their content. The recent passage of the Telecommunications Act with its 'v-chip' provision (see USA) has set the process going. (*Financial Post*)

CHINA

Scholars Chen Xiaoya, Yang Baiku, Zhou Yishan, and Chen Zhaogang were removed from their posts at the Chinese Academy of Social Sciences in early December in

Condemned ideas (for Wei Jingsheng)
by Yang Lian

Jailed dissident Wei Jingsheng was nominated by 81 US congressmen for the Nobel Peace Prize on 31 January. The Chinese Foreign Ministry reacted by saying Wei 'is a convicted criminal and therefore has no qualification to be awarded a Nobel prize.'

IN BEIJING, at the western end of Chang'an Avenue, billboards and construction sites cannot obscure a grey-coloured wall which lives in my memory — 'Democracy Wall', 1979 — crowds in grey-blue padded cotton jackets; youthful, emaciated faces; the dim street lights. Police cars parked at the mouths of the alleyways, the all-too-obvious plainclothesmen taking snapshots, silent farewells to the family before each meeting.

No, you're not a hero, you're just one of us. And what you said, 'There can be no Four Modernisations without democratic reform', that wasn't a prophecy, it was a simple fact, a fact whose image is blurred and faded in too many memories. But it was enough. As you yourself pointed out, if you push others to the point where they cannot avoid confrontation, you can't very well avoid such confrontation yourself. Prison is still waiting for you, 16 years after the great days of the Wall, 16 years which have seen the effacement and destruction of the ideas which you tried to establish.

I'm ashamed of myself. We have done nothing for

what is being seen as the start of a new anti-rightist campaign. All were involved in the 1989 pro-democracy movement — Yang and Chen Zhaogang were briefly imprisoned after the Tiananmen Square massacre, and Chen Xiaoya has recently published *The History of the 1989 Democracy Movement*. Their expulsion came after a secret conference in Xibobo, attended by commissars from the academy, held to discuss the growth of rightism in the party and in academic and media circles.

The campaign is believed to be being launched by the Communist Party's propaganda department and developed in leftist journals *The Mainstream* and *In Search of Truth*. Recent targets include philosopher Li Zehou, literary theorist Liu Zaifu, and writer Hu Jiwei. Scholars who attempt to revive traditional Chinese culture, such as Chen Ming, publisher of the neo-Confucianist journal *The Original Way*, have also been subject to official criticism. (*South China Morning Post*) you. There are only more bodies and more of the missing from Tiananmen Square, 4 June 1989. In the hopeless longing of their relatives, death itself is murdered once again by lies, while the movement's leaders, Chen Ziming and Wang Juntao, serve their 13-year sentences. The rest of the world delights in speaking of China's 'open-door reforms', but the only result is a two-year reduction in the penalty for 'thought-crimes'; although perhaps we should include the poets whose words can be broadcast at the will of the authorities, art exhibitions with official seals of approval, and books which have no readers. Ideas are all too concrete, to the point that the dictators believe that the ideas will wither away with the body; or, taking it a step further, the bodies will disappear along with the ideas. When they put you in prison, a piece of history is buried in silence. Every year in June, it's regiments of children who cover the great square of Tiananmen, who cover up the last faint traces of blood.

So, is that long, middle-aged face on the television really you? Facing a barred window for a second 14-year term, and smiling bravely. You know that you are facing a government which has humiliated the world. The world is humiliated precisely because it is without shame. Those two occasions on which it has shaken hands with the butchers, 1979 and 1989, they will not be forgotten. They will be remembered: power is that little bit more beautiful when it has been whitewashed twice over. Ideas silenced under the weight of a multi-billion dollar trade, this is as terrifying as a massacre, it too is murder. Expediency and duplicity, humankind's present trade in destruction, these have sealed your fate — and the fate of your ideas. You knew that your voice had to be silenced; if not, these crimes would never be secure.

This is 1996. When you come out of prison, a child born in 1979 will be 30 years of age, older than we were when we stood beside the Democracy Wall. How can we not feel ashamed? When your ideas have been ground down and refined by the stones of a dark prison, when you and your thoughts have become fact, then no-one will be able to avoid the necessary confrontation.

Yang Lian *is a poet and critic. He left China in 1989*
Translated by John Cayley

Four of the 15 signatories to a November petition calling for the release of Wei Jingsheng were detained in late December. The activists, Wang Donghai, Chen Longde, Fu Guoyong, and Wu Gaoxing, were detained on 27 December and held in 'Shelter and Investigation' until mid-January, when their sudden release coincided with the visit to China of a delegation from the US Congress. More dissidents were detained in China in 1995 than in any year since the pro-democracy crackdown of 1989. (Human Rights in China, Reuter)

According to a press edict issued by the Chinese State Council on 16 January, foreign news agencies are to come under the centralised control of Xinhua, the official Chinese news agency. Information groups, including Reuter, Dow Jones-Telerate, and Bloomberg, which sell economic news in China are required to register with Xinhua within three months and domestic organisations are forbidden to buy economic information directly from foreign sources. Xinhua will set the subscription rate for foreign vendors and those with information that 'slanders' China are threatened with punishment. Xinhua has defended the edict, which it describes as a move 'to safeguard state sovereignty' and 'protect the legal rights and interests of Chinese economic information users'. (International Press Institute, *International Herald Tribune*, *South China Morning Post*)

On 1 February new rules governing access to the Internet were issued. All companies providing access are now subject to official approval and all computer information networks are to use channels provided by the Ministry of Post and Telecommunications to link up to networks abroad. Any existing networks must disband and re-register. The ministry is installing filtering software to prevent the reception of material from foreign sources known to offer pornography or counter-revolutionary ideas. On 15 February Xinhua announced a further decree, under which all new users of international computer networks must register with the security forces within 30 days of linking to the network. (*Times, Guardian, Newsbytes News Network*)

Recent publications: *Death Penalty Continues to Expand in 1995* (AI, December 1995, 5pp); *Death by Default: A Policy of Fatal Neglect in China's State Orphanages* (HRW/Asia, January 1996, 394pp)

COLOMBIA

On 12 December Ernesto Acero Cadena, director of *Informador Socioeconomico* and a veteran reporter in the town of Quindio, was killed on the street by an unknown assailant. The 59-year-old journalist was known for his work in defence of press freedom. Authorities are looking into a possible connection between this murder and last year's disappearance and subsequent murder of Acero Cadena's son-in-law. (IAPA)

'Human rights! I don't understand'
'Me neither. It's all Chinese to me.'

COMOROS

On 6 January 1996, Youssof Moussa, editor of the government daily *El Watan*, was arrested and kept in detention for four days before being released on bail. A court order had been issued against Moussa and his colleague, Ben Abdullah, for attacking a judicial institution in connection with an article on judicial corruption. Following his release Moussa continued to publish similar articles. The public prosecutor responded on 25 January by banning *El Watan*. The order did not specify the duration of the ban, but allowed for 'military enforcement' of the ban if needed. (RSF)

COTE D'IVOIRE

Abou Drahamne Sangare, deputy leader of the opposition Ivorian Popular Front (FPI) and publisher of the Nouvel Horizon Group, and Emmanuel Kore, journalist for

La Voie, were sentenced to two years in prison and a fine of US$6,000 on 28 December. Kore's deputy, Freedom Neruda, was also sentenced to two years in prison on 11 January. *La Voie* was suspended for three months. It re-emerged, however, on 3 January under a new name, *L'Alternative*. Three journalists with *Le Republicain* were given three-month suspended sentences on 28 December, for defaming MP Moustapha Dinby. The paper was also banned for three months. (RSF)

CROATIA

In a 'state of the nation' speech to parliament on 15 January, President Franjo Tudjman warned that there is a need for greater regulation of the media since there has been 'irresponsible abuse of democratic rights', and 'the freedom of journalistic activity has not been co-ordinated with the necessity to provide legal protection for citizens as individuals, companies and state interests'. (SWB)

On 18 January the government ordered the independent station Radio LAE (*Index* 5/1995) to cease broadcasting immediately. The station's licence has been reassigned to Zeljko Paliska, an active member of the ruling Croatian Democratic Community (HDZ). A week later Igor Vukic and Kresimir Farkas, LAE's deputy manager and editor-in-chief respectively, were threatened with physical violence by two men believed to have been sent by Paliska and told to hand over LAE's transmitter. The same day the apartment of Dean Zahtila, LAE's general manager was burgled. Almost all available radio frequencies have been granted to groups close to the HDZ. (IFJ)

On 1 February it was reported that Ivan Parac has been replaced as director of Croatian Radio and TV by Ivica Mudrinic, a member of the governing HDZ, following a parliamentary vote. (OMRI, SWB)

CUBA

On 14 January poet and journalist Raul Rivero Castañeda and Juan Antonio Sánchez, both members of the independent agency Cuba Press, were arrested in Havana by security service agents. They were released the following day without charges but were warned to cease working for Cuba Press. Sánchez was arrested again on 17 February, together with his colleague Ana Luisa López Baeza. (*Le Monde*, AI, RSF)

On 19 January Luis Solar Hernández, a journalist with the Independant Cuban Press Bureau (BPIC), was detained by state security officers in Ciego de Avila. His address book and other personal belongings were confiscated and he was released the following day. Roxana Valdivia, also a BPIC journalist, was summoned to appear at state security offices for having violated orders not to receive dissidents in her home. (CPJ)

Police surrounded the BPIC offices in Havana on 15 February. They cut phone lines and prevented the journalists inside from leaving. The offices are in the home of Julio Restano and Aurora Díaz, the parents of BPIC founder Yndamiro Restano Díaz (*Index* 1/1995). The raid came nine days after Restano was awarded the International Federation of Newspaper Publishers' annual press freedom prize. A spokesperson for the agency, Norma Brito, was detained on 18 February. (CPJ, FIEJ, RSF)

Around 50 opposition activists were arrested in Havana between 15 and 19 February, among them Marta Beatriz Roque Cabello (*Index* 4/1995, p126) of the Cuban Institute of Independent Economists (IEIC). All the detainees are members of Concilio Cubano, an unofficial umbrella organisation of opposition groups. Concilio Cubano had been denied official permission to hold its national conference on 24 February. Roque was on her way to a meeting with the Italian ambassador, to seek assistance from the European Union in gaining permission for the conference, when she was arrested. Other detainees include Leonel Morejón Almagro, Néstor Rodríguez Lovaina of the Cuban Youth Movement for Democracy, Héctor Palacio Ruiz and Luis Zuñiga of the Democratic Solidarity Party. Roque and Morejón have gone on hunger strike in protest at the clampdown. (IEIC, Cubanet)

EGYPT

At least four journalists have received prison sentences and over 20 more face court cases on charges of libel under Law 93, the press law passed in May 1995 (*Index* 4/1995). Abdel al-Bakuri, editor-in-chief of weekly *al-Ahali*, and Sarouat Sourour, an *al-Ahali* journalist, were sentenced in absentia to two years' imprisonment and fined approximately US$15,000 after *al-Ahali* published a story about an allegedly corrupt police officer. Magdi Hussein (*Index* 3/1994, 1/1996), editor-in-chief of the Islamist *al-Sha'ab* newspaper, was sentenced on 31 January to a year's imprisonment with hard labour and fined US$4,500. In a separate case brought by a former minister over allegations of election fraud, Magdi Hussein faces a further charge of libel together with two other journalists, Mostafa Bakri, editor-in-chief of *al-Ahrar*, and Mahmoud Bakri of *Sout Helwan* and *al-Sha'ab*. On 17 February Mahmud al-Tohami, editor of the weekly *Rose al-Yussef*

(*Index* 1&2/1994), was sentenced to a year in prison for an article which accused a businessman of drug trafficking. In a report released on 8 February (see page 56) the Egyptian Organisation for Human Rights called for the press law to be amended and freedom of expression guaranteed. However, one member of the Journalists' Syndicate, Khaled Mohieddin, is using Law 93 to sue Ibrahim Issa, editor of weekly *al-Destour*, for libel after the publication named him as one of the '10 worst personalities' of 1995. (CPJ, RSF)

Recent publication: *The Copts of Egypt* by Saad Eddin Ibrahim, et al (Minority Rights Group International, January 1996, 30pp)

ESTONIA

An Estonian translation of the *Protocols of the Elders of Zion*, published in 1993, which was the subject of a court case in April 1995, continues to cause controversy. The Tartu city court found the publishers guilty of inciting nationalist and religious hatred and, in October, ordered the remaining 500 or so copies destroyed. The Executive Department, however, refused to burn the books on the grounds that they constitute 'court evidence'. The Jewish Community of Estonia argue that the book in its present form is 'inappropriate' and 'dangerous' since it is a straightforward facsimile of the 1934 edition, reprinted without commentary or explanation. They had not, however, asked for the books

to be destroyed. Nevertheless ,on 23 January police finally destroyed the remaining copies. (AP)

ETHIOPIA

Tesehalene Mengesha, deputy editor-in-chief of *Mebrook*; Mulugeta Lule, general manager of *Akpac* and *Tobiya*; Israel Saboqa, editor-in-chief and publisher of *Seife Nebelbal*; Garuma Bekele, general manager of *Urgi*; Lulit Gebre Mikael, editor-in-chief of the *Monitor*; and Iskinder Naga, editor-in-chief and publisher of *Habesha*, were all released between mid-November and the first week of January on bail of US$1,400. As of early January, the following remain in prison: Kassahun Tadesse, editor-in-chief of *Gananaw*; Dereje Birru, editor-in-chief of *Tequami*; Asseffa Beyene, editor-in-chief of *Ethiop*; Zerihun, newspaper distributor; Astor Agena, journalist with *Ethiop*; Alemu Lemma, executive editor-in-chief of *Beza*; Girmayeneh Mammo, executive editor-in-chief of *Tomma*; Solomon Lemma, executive editor-in-chief of *Wolafen*; Solomon Gebre Amlak, executive editor-in-chief of *Mogad* (now defunct); Andargue Mesfin, executive editor-in-chief of *Roha*; Terefe Mengesha, editor-in-chief of *Tenager*; Tedros Kebede, editor-in-chief of *Roha*; Getahun Bekele, editor-in-chief of *Tarik* and Sissay Agena, editor-in-chief of *Ethiop*. Agena was sentenced to a year's imprisonment in November for publishing a report that the central High Court deemed liable to incite civil unrest. The report in

question dealt with alleged losses by the army of the ruling Ethiopian People's Revolutionary Democratic Front. The court said that Agena was in breach of the press law, which bound him to ascertain the credibility of information before publishing it. (CPJ, SWB)

FRANCE

A quota law came into effect on 1 January, requiring all music radio stations to ensure that at least 40 per cent of the songs they play are French, and that half of them are newly released. (*Financial Times*)

The book *Le Grand Secret*, written by former president François Mitterrand's doctor Claude Gubler, was banned on 18 January, one day after publication, for violating medical confidentiality and privacy laws. The book alleges that Mitterrand concealed the extent of his terminal illness from the public and was physically unfit to govern during the last months of his presidency. On 24 January, however, the complete text of the book was posted on the Internet (http://www.le-web.fr/) by the owner of a cyber-café in Besançon. The ban applies only to the publisher and author of the book. (Reuter, Newsbytes News Network)

GERMANY

The US Internet provider CompuServe blacked out over 200 newsgroups containing sexually explicit material in January at the request of German authorities. On 13

February all but five of the newsgroups, which allegedly contain child pornography, were reinstated. (Reuter)

The national telephone company Deutsche Telekom AG blocked subscribers to its Internet service T-Online from accessing websites containing anti-Semitic material on 26 January. The move was prompted by a request from prosecutors in Mannheim who are investigating Ernst Zündel, a German émigré living in Canada who is well known for his persistent denial of the Holocaust. Internet users at three universities in the USA, where Zündel's website is based, responded by 'mirroring' the material on their own sites in protest at the ban, thereby making the Deutsche Telekom restriction irrelevant. (*Financial Post*)

GHANA

Cofi Coomson, editor of the country's leading independent paper, the *Ghanaian Chronicle*, was arrested on 9 February and charged with 'publishing false news with the intention of injuring the reputation of the state' in an article that implicated senior government members in a drugs and arms-trafficking case. Iben Quarcoo, editor of the bi-weekly *Free Press*, and the paper's publisher, Tommy Thompson, were arrested on similar charges on 12 February. The charges carry a maximum penalty of 10 years. (RSF, CPJ)

GUATEMALA

On the eve of the presidential election on 5 January, two members of the New Guatemalan Democratic Front were murdered in Totonicapán. Lucia Pu, who was eight months pregnant, was shot through the heart and her husband, Miguel Uz, was stabbed 20 times. (Reuter)

On 7 January a car bomb exploded outside the Washington home of José Pertierra, the lawyer of Jennifer Harbury (*Index* 3/1995). The following day, a bullet from a high-powered rifle was fired into Harbury's home. No-one has claimed responsibility for the attack but Pertierra accuses the Guatemalan army of trying to intimidate him and his client, who returned to Guatemala that week to exhume a mass grave in an army base, believed to contain the remains of her husband, Guatemalan guerrilla leader Efraín Bamaca. (*International Herald Tribune*)

On 1 February a historic court ruling ordered that soldiers accused of killing 11 returned refugees in October 1995 should be tried in a civilian rather than a military court. (SWB)

José Ruben Zamora, editor of the daily *Siglo Veintiuno*, has reported receiving a number of death threats in recent weeks. The paper's staff have been harassed repeatedly for reporting on military involvement in crime or corruption. The latest wave of threats appears to be connected to an interview the paper published on 2 February with a former military officer, now in exile, who implicated senior members of the army in crimes including massacres and kidnappings. (RSF, Reuter)

HAITI

Aharry Marsan, a Lavalas Party member of the Chamber of Deputies from Port au Piment, was shot twice in the face on 6 January near the Parliament building. (SWB)

On 10 January three people were wounded and a young girl was shot dead by National Police as peasants from Artibonite Valley blocked Route Nationale 1 with burning barricades in protest at power cuts that had prevented the use of vital irrigation pumps. The authorities have arrested one policeman although there have been no reports that he has been charged with any offence. (*Haiti Info*)

Six people were killed and hundreds left homeless after riots on 27 January in protest at the killing of Guy Jean-Pierre, a popular community leader in La Saline, Port-au-Prince. Three of those killed were stabbed and beaten in the belief that they were responsible for Jean-Pierre's death. (Reuter)

Recent publications: *Another Violence Against Women: The Lack of Accountability in Haiti* (Minnesota Advocates for Human Rights, December 1995, 24pp); *A Question of Justice* (AI, January 1996, 20pp)

HONDURAS

On 13 December seven people were injured and one was

killed when shots were fired at demonstrators at a summit of Central American presidents in San Pedro Sula. The demonstrators were protesting at the deaths of three people during a violent eviction (*Index* 1/1996). (Reuter)

The Honduran Appeals Court ruled on 5 January that 10 soldiers charged with the torture of students in 1982 are immune from prosecution under amnesty laws (*Index* 6/1995). (*Independent on Sunday*)

Journalist César Armando Pena, a correspondent for the radio station Voice of Honduras, was shot dead in Ocotopeque on 12 January by four men. Police arrested three of the men, while the fourth killed himself by detonating a grenade. (FIP)

HONG KONG

Democracy activists Lau Shan-ching, Leung Kwok-hung, and Yiu Yung-chin were refused 'home return permits' to enter China in late January, increasing fears of the existence of a Hong Kong blacklist. Yiu has applied repeatedly for a permit over the past three years but has always been rejected. Similar cases include that of newspaper columnist Paul Lin, denied entry in spite of a valid permit in 1992 and June 1995, and *Next* magazine photographer Tse Ming-chong, whose return permit was seized in Shenzhen. Earlier in January *Ping Kuo Jih Pao* (Apple Daily) quoted an anonymous Xinhua official who confirmed that some people were effectively barred

from entering China. (*South China Morning Post*, SWB)

HUNGARY

Parliament finally passed the new media bill on 21 December, with over 90 per cent of MPs voting in favour. The political row over the bill, which provides for privatisation of TV Channel 2 and Radio Danubius, and the operation of public service television and radio (including satellite Duna TV) as joint-stock companies run by public foundations, has been going on for several years. On 22 December the chairman of Hungarian TV, Adam Horvath, resigned in protest against the new law. (SWB)

It was reported on 16 January that, under the new broadcasting laws, membership of the controlling national radio and television body will be subject to 'incompatibility rules'. This means that members of national or local government, MPs, senior members of political parties' executives, management or personnel of broadcasting companies, and proprietors and shareholders of such companies cannot serve on the body. (SWB)

INDIA

A painting by Dutch artist Rob Birza hanging in the National Gallery of Modern Art, New Delhi, was vandalised by nationalists at the beginning of January. The painting included a slogan which could be read both as 'Kill India' and 'Kiss India'. The artist said this means that the forces of love

would conquer the forces of hatred in India. Nationalists interpreted it as an insult by western enemies of India. The gallery management denied that the painting had been permanently removed. In the past the management has been criticised for exhibiting homoerotic paintings by Bhupen Khakhar in a separate room. (*Guardian*)

Customs officials were reported at the end of January to have prohibited a book on Kashmir from entering the country. *Reclaiming the Past? The Search for Political and Cultural Unity in Contemporary Jammu and Kashmir*, by Vernon Hewitt, is critical of both Pakistan and India. The Home Ministry has issued a standing order that any book on Kashmir be sent to them by booksellers before release. (*Outlook*)

The film *Bandit Queen*, based on the life of dacoit Phoolan Devi, was banned in the city of Aurangabad for two months from 9 February, because of 'chances of a breach of public order'. Women's groups, art critics and other interest groups have called for the film to be banned outright because of its frank depiction of sex and violence. (*The Hindu*)

Following a ruling by the Supreme Court that the airwaves are public property and should not be monopolised by the state, the government is considering a new law permitting private radio and television stations. It is not clear when the bill will be put before Parliament. (Reuter)

INDONESIA

On 18 December journalist Meirizal Zulkarnain was dismissed from his job with *Bisnis Indonesia*. He is thought to have been sacked because of his links with the unofficial Alliance of Independent Journalists (AJI). (A19)

On 12 January the Press Council agreed to allow broadsheet daily newspapers to expand to 24 pages and tabloid papers to 48 pages. The previous maximum was 20 pages, with advertising occupying not more than a third of the total. The restriction had been seen as necessary to enable provincial papers to compete with the large Jakarta newspapers. (*Jakarta Post*)

The Portuguese state television station, RTP-International, began broadcasting to East Timor on 28 January. The first broadcast carried a speech from the Portuguese prime minister, Antonio Guterres, in the Timorese language Tetum. 'It is necessary to support your wish for freedom, your right to self-determination and your fight for respect for human rights,' he said. Portugal is still regarded by the UN as the administering power in East Timor. (Reuter, SWB)

Recent publications: *Women in Indonesia and East Timor: Standing Against Repression* (AI, December 1995, 23pp); *Journalists' Sentences are Increased as Media Restrictions Continue* (AI, December 1995, 15pp)

IRAN

Abolgassem Golbaf, publisher of the monthly *Gozaresh* (Report), was sentenced to three months in prison on 26 December after being found guilty of 'publishing lies' about a fertiliser firm run by the Ministry of Agriculture. The court said it took account of Golbaf's 'tone and the unpleasantness of his defence statement' in determining the sentence. (Reuter)

Police raided 110 homes in Tehran on 8 January and seized illegal satellite television equipment. Dishes have started reappearing in Tehran in recent months, in violation of a ban brought in in April last year (*Index* 3/1995). (Reuter)

Exiled poet Siavoush Kasrai died in Vienna on 8 February. He faced repression both under the regime of the Shah and after the 1979 revolution, going into exile in 1982. His last book of poems, *Mohrey-e Sorkh* (The Red Prawn), was published in Vienna in 1995. (Iranian PEN Centre in Exile)

ISRAEL

Israeli media have called for reform of censorship laws following the widespread reporting of the appointment on 9 January of Rear-Admiral Ami Ayalon as the new head of the secret service agency, Shin Bet. The reports printed Ayalon's full name in apparent breach of present legal restrictions. He replaces Karmi Gilon, who resigned on 8 January and who the media were permitted to refer to only as Kaf, the Hebrew initial of his first name, despite his full name being published in foreign publications and his address posted on the Internet. Quoting foreign news reports about his resignation, newspapers published Gilon's full name and a photograph. (*Financial Times*)

Amer Jaabari, a cameraman for US television network ABC, was beaten and arrested by Israeli soldiers while covering a demonstration in Hebron in the West Bank on 19 January. (RSF)

Sha'wan Rateb Jabarin, fieldworker for the human rights organisation Al Haq, was arrested by the General Security Service (GSS) on 5 February and has been sentenced to six months' administrative detention without charge or trial. He had been working with Article 19, the International Commission of Jurists and Al Haq in a joint project monitoring freedom of expression and human rights

The monotony of lies

by Goenawan Mohamad

One year after the arrests of Eko Maryadi, Ahmad Taufik and Danang Wardoyo of Independen, *and Tri Agus Susanto of* Kabar dari Pijar, *the editor of the banned news weekly* Tempo, *reflects on the price of speaking out*

TODAY in Indonesia, four young men are still behind bars, after being indicted of a peculiar kind of crime, namely because they published news stories the government did not want to be printed.

Let me describe briefly what their alleged crime was. One of them, a person of great courage, quoted a statement by a famous human rights lawyer lambasting President Suharto for banning *Tempo* — and he wrote the story in an unlicensed bulletin his organisation issued. Two of them, guilty of 'spreading hatred and heaping abuses upon the government', are members of the new journalists' union called the Alliance of Independent Journalists (AJI). They were involved with the publication of another unlicensed journal, printing, among other things, a story about the large number of media owned personally and illegally by the minister of information. The fourth is a boy of barely 19, an employee in the AJI office, who was sentenced to 20 months in jail for helping the journalists.

What they did was to insist that the press and society should give priority to freedom. Given the current political economy of the media, in which government and/or business interests are the ones that overwhelmingly rule the roost, the insistence on journalistic freedom is at the same time the insistence on journalistic responsibility.

To be responsible one has to be free. Parrots and robots cannot claim responsibility for whatever they say and do, because they just copy and follow others' words. This is an important point to stress, since the most often-used apology for censorship tends to pit the idea of freedom against the idea of responsibility. To be sure, there are ethical considerations a journalist has to be aware of every time he writes and gets published. But the substance of ethics is self-restraint (the emphasis is on 'self'). It necessarily presupposes freedom. What one ought to do and not do is decided in the solitude of

during the Palestinian elections. This is the sixth administrative detention order imposed on Jabarin since 1987. (A19)

Moshe Vardi, editor-in-chief of *Yedioth Ahronoth* and his deputy, will be charged with wiretapping staff at *Ma'ariv*, the rival newspaper (see page 65). *Ma'ariv's* editor, Ofer Nimrodi, is already on trial for ordering wiretaps against *Yedioth* (*Index* 5/1995). (AP)

ITALY

The BBC's Arabic-language service, which is relayed to the Middle East from Rome, was blacked out from 5 January at any mention during news broadcasts of the threatened deportation of Saudi dissident Mohammed al-Mas'ari (see United Kingdom, below). The relay station is owned by Prince Khalid bin Abdallah, a cousin of Saudi Arabia's King Fahd. (*Guardian*)

JAPAN

Businessman Hiroshi Kamekura was arrested in Tokyo in January on suspicion of distributing pornography on his home page on the World Wide Web in what is believed to be the first case of its kind in Japan. Kamekura had displayed pornographic images on the Web since December. Police raided both his home and the offices of the Internet provider who supplied him with one's independence. That's why it is absurd to let governments and media proprietors hold all the cards in determining the parameters of journalistic ethics.

Of course, in many countries in Asia, the press is by no means equivalent to the fourth estate. Politically, the media — especially the print media — do not yet belong to the big league. When election results are either rigged or illegally collected, when public opinion is often generated by oral communication (with various degrees of brainwashing), and not by an elegant piece of prose on the editorial page, when average circulation figures are very low, the press can only have a very limited claim on political life and its changes. To borrow Anthony Sampson's description of British journalism, one can say that many newspapers in Asia are not the extension of history but of conversation.

Still, it is an important piece of public conversation. At least it can raise, or give room to, pertinent questions, opposing views and perspectives, and challenge the monotony of lies. In a society where the ruling elite tends to dictate the style and the substance of discourse, the so-called harmony — a highly valued thing in Asian societies, they say — tends to silence the weak.

Journalists and the mass media may not change this overnight. In many countries in Asia, the press is not a powerful political player. But I like to think that their submissive and weak appearance is like that of water. 'In the world there is nothing more submissive and weak than water. Yet for attacking that which is hard and strong nothing can surpass it.'

That is a quote from Lao-tze.

connection services. A high school student accused of distributing pornography since September is also under investigation. (Newsbytes News Network)

JORDAN

Ali Udaybat, chief editor of weekly *Sawt al-Mar'ah*, was charged on 15 December with insulting the head of a foreign state and disturbing relations between Jordan and Iraq. The

charges came after the newspaper published an article on 18 October, which was deemed offensive by Iraqi president Saddam Hussein. The complaint against the editor was filed by the Press and Publications Department at the instigation of the Iraqi ambassador in Amman. Also in December Fahd al-Rimawi, editor-in-chief of *al-Majd*, was charged with disturbing relations between Jordan and Bahrain, following an article in

February last year which called on Bahrain to follow Jordan's model of 'Arabisation'. The case was brought after a complaint by the Bahraini Emiri court. (SWB)

KENYA

Photojournalist Njenga Munyori was found murdered in Kiambu district, central Kenya, on 21 December. He had been working with Interlink Rural Information Service at the time of his death and had previously worked for the Nation group of newspapers. (*NGAO*)

President Moi banned *Family Life*, an American Girl Guides Association book on 1 January, because it discusses sex. The book is 'immoral' and 'promotes promiscuity' said Moi. (Reuter)

In a speech on 26 January President Moi announced that the proposed media laws (*Index* 1/1996) have been shelved, saying they had been misunderstood and that the government had never had any intention of muzzling the press. This move came after considerable pressure from international press freedom organisations, whose criticism President Moi subsequently condemned as 'uncalled-for and malicious'. (Reuter)

Lawyers for jailed opposition politician Koigi wa Wamwere (*Index* 2/1995, 6/1995) expressed concern in February at continued delays in a date being granted for his appeal and bail hearing. After a deeply flawed trial, wa Wamwere was sentenced to four years in

'Our sentence was a disguised death sentence'

by Koigi wa Wamwere

The British government is considering adding Kenya to the 'White List' of countries from which asylum requests will not be considered. Here, Koigi wa Wamwere — who narrowly escaped the death sentence last year — describes life in a Kenyan top-security prison

To comprehend fully the harshness of a four-year sentence, one must understand that conditions in Kenyan prisons are so brutal that one does not need a death sentence to die in prison. In fact, while hundreds of prisoners are sentenced to hang in Kenya each year, many, many more prisoners die each year unconvicted and unsentenced to die by courts of law.

Sometime back, a Kenyan judge described our prisons as 'death chambers'. There are many prisoners who die after being put into these death chambers for just one or two months. A prison warder told me recently that once, overcrowding in Nairobi Remand Prison was so bad that it was killing an average of 15 prisoners a day! Now, if conditions in these death chambers are bad enough to kill a prisoner after only two or three months, what chance of survival has one who has been put into these death chambers to play hide-and-seek with death for a whole 72 months?...

In prison we must buy all our own drugs, or die of untreated diseases, as many prisoners have already done. To buy our drugs, we must be lucky enough to fall sick when our relatives are about to come to visit, and buy our drugs for us. If we fall sick when a visit is far off, or when relatives have no money, we shall be as good as dead.

Because prisoners are given no soap, toilet paper or toothpaste, those whose relatives cannot buy those things for them are kept in a state of great filth. Imagine, prisoners are forced to use pages of the Bible or pieces of blanket as toilet paper.

prison, six strokes of the cane and five years' deprivation of full civil rights in October last year. He is currently being held in Kamiti Maximum Security Prison. (PEN)

Recent publication: *Torture Compounded by the Denial of Medical Care* (AI, December 1995, 29pp)

LIBERIA

The Information Ministry announced on 27 December that the Press Union of Liberia (PUL) is no longer authorised to accredit journalists. It gave journalists 10 days to register with the ministry or risk being barred from covering public functions. (SWB)

On 9 January James Seitua, editor-in-chief of the *Daily Observer*, was arrested in connection with an article, printed on 29 December that alluded to supposed links between rebels in Sierra Leone and the main Liberian faction, the National Patriotic Front of Liberia. He was later charged with 'criminal malevolence' and released on bail. Stanton Peabody, also of the *Daily Observer*, was arrested on 10 January when he went to Monrovia police headquarters to intervene on behalf of Seitua. Meanwhile, staff at the offices of the *Inquirer* newspaper prevented police from arresting production manager Jacob Doe on 11 January. The attempted arrest stemmed from a front-page article printed that day, which criticised the arrests of Seitua and Peabody. (Reuter)

On 15 January seven independent newspapers and four independent radio stations called a 24-hour press blackout to protest against continued harassment of independent journalists by the security forces (CPJ)

Dirt and lack of water are not just bad in themselves. They breed vermin, like bedbugs and lice. In fact, prisoners' main preoccupation in their spare time is picking lice from their clothes and killing them. But lice become so numerous that trying to kill them is a useless exercise. One time I saw a prisoner whose clothes were so completely covered by swarms of lice, there were layers and layers of them. And when it was warm and they began moving, the man just became a pillar of moving lice...

Prisoners are flogged with special canes that cut the flesh but don't break when they strike a man's buttocks. The canes are imported from Singapore, where they are specially grown for flogging and making swagger-canes for officers in the armed forces. But in prison swagger-canes are randomly used for caning prisoners as a punishment for petty offences, like talking back to an officer, stealing food, keeping one's hands in one's pockets, being in possession of contraband such as cigarettes, sugar, or a newspaper...

Before a prisoner is caned, a doctor must examine him and declare him fit for caning. Once a prisoner has been certified fit, his hands, thighs and waist are pinned with handcuffs to a triangular stand, like the ones used in building sites. His buttocks are then pasted with a piece of blanket which has been soaked in thick salt water.

The cane, too, is soaked in salt water for five days, to make it pliable and tough. When the cane strikes the buttocks, it cuts deeply into the flesh and salt water from the blanket seeps into the fresh wound causing such pain that the victim will often vomit and faint. It is also said that striking the buttocks forces the victim to ejaculate involuntarily. After caning, the buttocks will be grooved with raw, deep wounds that take weeks and months to heal. When a prisoner is healing, he has to lie on his stomach all the time, because he cannot sit...

Excerpted from a handwritten 260-page manuscript to be published in May by Norwegian publishers Aschehoug, who also publish wa Wamwere's A Dream of Freedom. *For information about publishing rights contact Aschehoug on 47-22 400 400 or halfdan.freihow@aschehoug.no*

LIBYA

Twenty-four students who took part in demonstrations last year are believed to have been tortured while in al-Jdayda Prison, outside Tripoli. Arrested after demonstrations in Bani Walid last September, the students were reportedly tried in secret and sentenced to between two and nine years' imprisonment. (AI, Reuter)

MACEDONIA

On 16 December the illegal Albanian-language university (*Index* 1/1995) celebrated its first anniversary. Despite government attempts to shut the university down, it reportedly runs underground faculties in science, the humanities, economics and law. (OMRI)

On 4 February radio and television director-general Melpomeni Korneti sacked Saso Ordanoski, director of Macedonian television, accusing him of disrupting scheduled programming and a lack of objectivity. The television editorial board criticised the dismissal as contrary to the principles of press freedom and on 5 February minister without portfolio Ismail Gjuner resigned in protest, saying that Ordanoski had been good for Macedonian journalism and democracy. (OMRI)

MALAYSIA

Information minister Mohamed Rahmat said on 27 January that entertainers who were caught taking drugs would be banned from the airwaves. The warning came the day after rock singer Saleem was arrested by police during an anti-dug raid. The singer Jamal Abdullah has already been blacklisted from radio and television after being convicted for drug offences. (*Straits Times*)

The state of Kelantan, ruled by the fundamentalist PAS, has said that it is looking into the possibility of closing down cinemas in the state. A spokesman said the proposal would be used 'as a last resort' if the state found no other way to curb the 'adverse effects' of films shown in the cinemas. (*Guardian, Straits Times*)

State-run Radio-Television Malaysia announced that the popular children's television programme *Mighty Morphin' Power Rangers* may be broadcast in Malaysia only if the word 'morphin' is deleted. The programme was taken off the air because the word sounds too much like the drug morphine. The show's producer, Nick Larkin, said the word was 'morphing' without the 'g'. 'It's short for metamorphosing,' he explained. (Reuter)

MALDIVES

Mohamed Latheef, linguist, Ahamed Shafeeq, former civil servant, and Ali Moosa Didi, writer and politician, were all released from house arrest on 31 December on the condition that they do not leave the capital, Male. They were arrested on 21 April 1995. According to an article published in *Haveeru* and *Aafathison* on 1 January, they are accused of publishing articles and books 'violating the good name and greatness of the Maldivian people' and of endangering national security. There were further accusations of making

degrading allegations against the head of state, and of attempting to weaken the state through 'their talking and thinking'. (AI)

MAURITANIA

The 10 January edition of daily *Mauritanie-Nouvelles* was seized at the presses on the order of the Interior Ministry under Article 11 of the press law. Managing editor Bah Ould Saleck was accused by the ministry of 'defaming the police' in December and has been repeatedly summoned to police headquarters for questioning. The entire print run of the 5 February edition of the paper was also seized, apparently because of an interview with a Mauritanian opposition leader based in Senegal who urged the use of force to overthrow the government. (RSF)

MAURITIUS

Namassiwayam Ramalingum, editor of the weekly *L'Indépendant*, continues to be persecuted by Islamists. Since a *fatwa* was issued against him in May 1995 (*Index* 3/1995), he has remained in hiding and his offices closed. The Mauritian authorities and police have yet to take any action in providing protection for him, despite repeated requests to do so. (CPJ)

MEXICO

The owners and editor of *El Mañana*, a daily paper in Nuevo Laredo, Tamaulipas, reported receiving death threats in January. They have also been subject to other

forms of intimidation, such as distribution boycotts and the freezing of government sources of information. On 13 February Raymundo Ramos, a reporter for the paper, was approached by two unidentified men and warned to stop writing critical articles about the state government. (IAPA, CPJ)

On 12 January Rocío Culebro, co-ordinator of the National Network of Non-Governmental Human Rights Organisations, received a number of threatening phone calls. The next day Culebro was due to travel to the Inter-American Commission on Human Rights in order to present the organisation's third report on the massacre of 17 peasants at Aguas Blancas, Guerrero state. (AI)

Lourdes Figuérez, a researcher at the Bi-National Centre for Human Rights (CBDH), received death threats on 15 January at the organisation's office in Tijuana, Baja California. Since September 1995 CBDH has been working on a case of the alleged torture of five youths by three members of the State Judicial Police (PJE) in Tijuana. At their trial the three PJE members were found guilty and the court called for their dismissal. The CBDH has documented 425 cases of torture in Baja California, but this is the first time that the organisation has been able bring PJE members to justice. (AI)

Recent publication: *Massacre in Mexico: Killings and Cover-up in the State of Guerrero* (Minnesota

Advocates for Human Rights, December 1995, 33pp)

MOLDOVA

On 7 February Parliament voted down an amendment to the 1994 Press Law (*Index* 6/1994). The amendment would have revoked the ban on publishing documents that 'criticise or defame the state and its people' and removed sanctions for 'attacks on personal dignity'. (RSF)

MOROCCO

The 28 January edition of the newspaper *Anwal* was confiscated by the authorities, apparently because it had resumed serialisation of the book *The Moroccan Monarchy and the Struggle for Power* by Maati Mounjib, without waiting for permission from the Interior Ministry. The ministry had temporarily withdrawn permission because, it said, the book contained inaccuracies. However, *Anwal*'s editorial staff decided that the book was accurate and that serialisation should continue. (RSF, A19)

A one-man show, 'Water on Sand' by satirist Ahmed Senoussi, also known as Bziz (*Index* 1/1995), scheduled for 8 February, was banned by the Interior Ministry on the grounds that it would be a 'threat to public order'. Senoussi's shows cover current events and parody government figures. (Reuter)

NEW ZEALAND

A report reviewing the Office of Film and Literature

Classification's first year of operation concluded that the government would have to treble its expenditure to NZ$7.4 million per year to mount an effective roadblock against pornography on the Internet. It was suggested that the increase could be funded partly by increasing classification charges for books and magazines from $100 to $600, and for CD-Roms from $600 to $1,050. (*National Business Review*)

A photography exhibition featuring sexually explicit works by US photographer Robert Mapplethorpe drew street protests at its New Zealand opening. The exhibition had been cancelled in Washington DC, USA, a gallery director was arrested in Cincinnati, Ohio, USA, and in Wellington a censor rated the show suitable for people only over 18. On 15 December a nine-day-old baby was refused entry to the exhibition when taken by his mother. (Reuter, *Times*)

NICARAGUA

Professor Porifirio Ramos died and 35 students were injured when police opened fire on a demonstration outside the National Assembly on 13 December. The protesters were demanding that President Chamorro's government honour a constitutional provision allocating six per cent of the national budget to education. (*Mesoamerica*)

NIGER

Several journalists have been arrested or threatened in the

wake of the January coup against President Mahamane Ousame. Moulaye Abdoulaye, managing director of the daily *Le Soleil*, was arrested and beaten on 6 February. The paper was a close supporter of President Ousame. On 10 February soldiers went to the homes of Moussa Shangari and Ibrahim Hamidou, managing directors respectively of *L'Alternative* and *La Tribune du Peuple*, apparently to arrest them. Both men were out at the time, and neither has been seen since. Since the coup, the High Council for Communications, which is meant to guarantee opposition access to state media, has been abolished. (RSF)

NIGERIA

Nosa Igiebor, editor-in-chief of *Tell* magazine, was arrested by State Security Service Agents (SSSA) on 23 December. Since then he has

Recent publication:
A Month and a Day
Ken Saro-Wiwa's prison diaries, Penguin Books,
£6.99/US$10.95

been detained incommunicado and reportedly denied medication for hypertension and an ulcer. On 30 January Chief Gani Fawehinmi, attorney for Igiebor and for *Tell*, was also picked up by SSSA at his home in Lagos. During December the authorities raided the magazine's offices at least twice and confiscated over 55,000 copies of recent editions. Vendors have also been harassed for selling the magazine. (CPJ)

Posters threatening the life of Nobel laureate Wole Soyinka appeared in Lagos in early January, two days after a government minister accused him of involvement in bomb attacks in Kano and Kaduna. A copy of one of Soyinka's books was found in a hotel room used by the bomber. (*Guardian*)

On 2 February Alex Ibru, publisher of the *Guardian*, sustained gunshot wounds to his head and left hand when he was shot at point-blank range in his car on his return home from his office. Police say the motive for the attack was robbery, but nothing was stolen from Ibru's car. (CPJ, Reuter)

Hillary Anderson, the BBC's new Lagos correspondent, was detained by the SSSA on 15 February, one week after arriving to take up her post. She was released 24 hours later. No reason was given for her detention. (CPJ)

A further 19 Ogoni activists are being held in Port Harcourt Prison charged with the same murders for which Ken Saro-Wiwa and eight others were hanged in November (*Index* 1/1996). Sixteen of those detained are supporters of the Movement for the Survival of the Ogoni People (MOSOP): Elijah Baadom, John Banatu, Kagbara Basseh, Israel Blessing, Friday Gburuma, Paul Deekor, Godwin Gbodoo, Adam Kaan, Bariture Lebee, Nyieda Nasikpo, Sampson Ntignee, Nwinbari Abere Papa, Pogbara Zorzor, Samuel Asigha, Barbina Visor, Benjamin Kabari. The three others have been named as Taagalo Monsi, Baribuma Kumanwe and Ngbaa Baovi. (AI, *Guardian*)

Recent publication: *A Travesty of Law and Justice: An Analysis of the Judgement in the Case of Ken Saro-Wiwa and Others* by Michael Birnbaum QC (A19, December 1995, 21pp)

PAKISTAN

There have been repeated attacks on the Sindhi-language paper *Kawish* in recent months. On 20 December activists from the Sindhi nationalist Jeay Sindh Tarraqi Pasand Party (JSTPP) ransacked the Sukkur and Larkana offices and threatened the bureau chiefs. On 23 December five armed men attacked the Karachi office. On 22 and 23 December copies of the paper were publicly burned in 13 cities across Sindh province, and vendors threatened. The attacks came after a report accusing nationalist parties of extorting money from local people. In separate incidents, the Karachi offices of the Sindhi-language daily *Ibrat*

were attacked on 9 January; and on 11 February Monis Bokhari, correspondent for the daily *Sindh* in Dokri, was arrested and severely beaten by local police. (Pakistan Press Foundation)

PALESTINE (GAZA-JERICHO)

Maher al-Alami, a senior editor at the Arabic-language daily *al-Quds*, was summoned for questioning in Jericho on 25 December and held for six days, apparently because he had refused Yasser Arafat's request to place a certain story on the front page. The story, about the Greek Orthodox patriarch granting Arafat symbolic custody of Christian holy sites in Jerusalem, was printed on page eight. On 2 January Bassem Eid, a journalist and fieldworker for B'Tselem, the Jerusalem-based human rights organisation, and Reporters Sans Frontières, was taken by Palestinian security forces from his home in East Jerusalem - an area where the PNA has no jurisdiction - and held for 24 hours in Ramallah in the West Bank. No reason for his arrest was given but on release Bassem Eid claimed that his arrest was part of a deliberate policy to silence critics of Arafat in the run-up to the elections on 20 January. (Palestinian Media Monitoring Centre)

Police closed the offices of the Islamic Jihad newspaper *al-Istiqlal* until further notice on 18 February and arrested the editor, Alaa Saftawi (*Index* 5/1995). The arrest stemmed from an editorial about Yasser Arafat's swearing-in as elected president, which said: 'He may make mistakes or terrorise the people, but God will not forgive him. Taking an oath on the Quran is a serious responsibility.' (RSF)

Recent publications: *Critique of the Press Law 1995 Issued by the Palestinian Authority* (Palestinian Centre for Human Rights, Series Study 1, 52pp, Series Study 2, 63pp. Available from: Qadada Building, PO Box 1204, Omar al Mukhtar Street, Gaza City, Gaza Strip, tel +9727 825893, fax +9727 824776); *Health Services: One Year After Transfer to the Palestinian Authority* (Physicians for Human Rights, November 1995, 48pp); *Freedom of the Press under the Palestinian Authority* (Peace Watch, January 1996, 40pp)

PHILIPPINES

Ferdinand Reyes, a human rights lawyer and editor of the weekly *Press Freedom*, was shot dead by a lone gunman in his office in Dipolog City on 12 February. The killer fled with an accomplice on a motorcycle. Reyes was a prominent campaigner against corruption and human rights abuses by the military, and had received death threats in the past. His murder came three days after he led a small rally against new anti-terrorism legislation. (RSF, CPJ)

POLAND

Prime minister Jozef Oleksey, accused of being a former spy for the KGB, attacked Polish television and its head Wieslaw Walendziak on 23 January for making it 'impossible' for him

to defend himself against the allegations. Walendziak denies that the Oleksey has been denied airtime, saying that he was entitled to it, but had not requested it. Five days previously, the Polish Journalists' Association wrote to the Sejm speaker, Jozef Zych, asking for the proceedings of the Sejm special commission investigating the allegations to be made public, saying that public opinion is being kept 'insufficiently informed'. (SWB)

Jerzy Urban, editor-in-chief of the satirical weekly *Nie* (No), was fined US$4,000 and barred from managing a publication or working as a journalist for one year on 6 February, after being found guilty of publishing classified documents (see over). The charge arose from a 1992 article in *Nie* which contained extracts from the former Communist political police archive. Urban was also given a one-year suspended sentence. (CPJ)

ROMANIA

The National Audiovisual Council released broadcasting guidelines for coverage of the April general elections on 16 January. All candidates will have free and equal access to the media and material slandering political opponents will be banned. No opinion polls may be published in the run-up to the election. The regulations will also apply to the presidential elections due at the end of the year. (OMRI)

On 6 February the Senate endorsed a bill placing the

Foreign Intelligence Service (SIE), which deals with counter-intelligence, under parliamentary control. The SIE will be responsible to the Supreme Defence Council headed by President Iliescu. The bill has still to be debated by the Chamber of Deputies. (Reuter, OMRI)

RUSSIAN FEDERATION

Russia: Parliamentarian Anatoly Shabad was seriously injured in a hit-and-run accident on 11 December while on his way to a public meeting at the Izvestiya office in Moscow. Shabad is one of the most outspoken critics of the Russian army's Chechnya campaign. He believes that the incident was a deliberate attempt on his life. (*Express-Chronicle*)

Sergei Grigoryants, chairman of the organising committee of the International Public Tribunal on Chechnya, was detained with two colleagues at Moscow airport on 15 December as they were about to leave for the tribunal's hearings in Stockholm. Books, computer disks, videotapes and documents were confiscated. (*Express-Chronicle*)

Molotov cocktails were thrown through the windows of the offices of the daily *Russki Sever* (North of Russia) in Vologda, northeast Russia, on 24 December. A driver for a losing candidate in the 17 December elections said he received US$20 in exchange for setting fire to the paper's offices. The newspaper had supported the successful candidate. (RSF)

No to *Nie*

by Vera Rich

THE JERZY URBAN case has caused considerable public comment in Poland. He was charged with revealing state secrets, among them an undertaking to co-operate with the secret police, signed in 1958 by Zdzislaw Najder, who later became director of the Polish section of Radio Free Europe and, in the post-Communist era, an adviser to then-premier Jan Olszewski.

The fact that the defendant was Jerzy Urban adds a peculiar piquancy. This is not the first time that Urban has been banned from the press scene. His first journalistic post, in 1955-57, was with the revisionist Communist youth journal *Po Prostu*. This was closed down on the order of the reformist party leader Wladyslaw Gomulka in 1957, and its staff forbidden to work as journalists. Urban survived for a time on freelance work and then, in 1968, joined the Agencja Robotnicza (Workers News Agency). From this, in 1962, he went on to the prestigious weekly *Polityka*, where he worked almost continuously until December 1981 when, with the declaration of martial law by General Wojciech Jaruzelski, he was co-opted as government media spokesman.

During his eight years in this post a considerable part of his work consisted in denying and attacking precisely the kind of leak covered by the law under which he has just been sentenced. On at least two occasions his zeal proved embarrassing: on one occasion he mistakenly cited the BBC's Warsaw correspondent as the author of disinformation concerning regulations on Polish scientists wishing to travel abroad. The Academy of Sciences pointed out that the regulations were in fact being applied — although the BBC correspondent was not the source of the leak. On another occasion, he accused a group of academics of being in touch with a CIA controller at the US embassy in Warsaw, a charge for which he was obliged to make a public apology. One of the accused, Janusz Onyszkiewicz, later became Poland's first civilian minister of defence in the post-totalitarian era.

In April 1989, at the time of the 'round table' which eventually led to multi-party elections, Urban became minister of information but in September he was recalled and became director of the Krajowa Agencja Robotnicza (All-Poland Workers News Agency). Shortly afterwards, he went on to found the satirical/sensationalist *Nie* (No), and in December 1991 sponsored the Nie movement, which described itself as an association opposing all forms of intolerance and dictatorship, nationalism, populism and totalitarianism and, in particular, the introduction of a new code of medical ethics forbidding abortion.

Urban's variegated history provoked a number of comments during the trial. The magistrate, Pawel Rysinski, pointed out that, as a former government press spokesman and minister of information, Urban could hardly claim ignorance of the law. He also said it is not the role of a journalist to publish secret documents. Najder himself, who appeared in court as a witness, denied ever having denounced anyone to the secret police, but said that he had already publicly acknowledged that he had had contact with them in the past. 'It is grotesque', he said, 'that he [Urban] should come forward as a 'cleanser' of people's pasts. How can he think of unmasking people connected with Communism when he himself co-operated with them?'

Oleg Slabynko, producer of the television programme *Moment of Truth*, was shot dead outside his apartment on 25 January. There are suspicions that his murder may be connected with the murder last year of Vladislav Listyev (*Index* 2/1995). (Reuter)

Since 12 February, government officials have banned journalists from NTV, the country's only independent television station, from covering events at the Kremlin. NTV officials believe the ban is connected with an interview it broadcast with Vyacheslav Kostikov, President Yeltsin's former press secretary. (CPJ)

Chechnya: Shakhman Kagirov, of the Moscow-based paper *Rossiyskaya Gazeta* and the Chechen government's paper *Vozrozhdeniye*, was shot dead by Chechen militants in an ambush near Grozny on 13 December. (SWB)

Dagestan: Several foreign and local journalists covering the hostage crisis in Dagestan were harassed or fed misinformation by Russian authorities in the area. On 10 January reporters were kept away from Kizlyar, where the hostages were first taken. Security officials eventually granted access to a restricted group of reporters. After the hostages were taken to Pervomayskoye, Worldwide Television News producer Grigori Kouznetsov and cameraman Nikolai Chichkov, who had gained entry to the village, were detained by Russian troops and had their equipment confiscated. On 16 January a

crew from the American Broadcasting Corporation were attacked by guard dogs as they tried to pass a checkpoint five miles from the village. The same day a *New York Times* reporter was shot at by soldiers in a Russian military jeep as he tried to drive through the checkpoint. And Peter Ford, a reporter for the *Christian Science Monitor*, was badly bitten by a guard dog at the same checkpoint earlier in the day. (CPJ, RSF)

RWANDA

The first three Rwandans to be prosecuted for genocide by the International Criminal Tribunal for Rwanda were named on 12 January. The three suspects are the former mayors of Muganza and Goma and Alphonse Higaniro, the former transport and communications minister, all of whom are currently being held in Belgium. On 31 January the tribunal formally protested to the authorities after three of its investigators were beaten by Rwandan soldiers. (Reuter, *Guardian, International Herald Tribune*)

SERBIA-MONTENEGRO

Serbia: On 9 January the government formally requested Parliament's Cultural Committee to make management changes at the state-run corporation Radio and TV Serbia and presented a list of candidates which included prominent members of the ruling Socialist Party of Serbia (SPS) and its political allies and sympathisers. Opposition parties criticised the request as another attempt

to secure the ruling party's dominant position in the media. (OMRI)

On 1 February police prevented five opposition parties from meeting as an 'alternative legislature' in the parliament building. The parties — the Serbian Renewal Movement, the Radical Party, the Democratic Party, the Democratic Party of Serbia and the Democratic Community of Hungarians in Vojvodina — had set up the 'alternative legislature' in December in protest at the Socialist Party's heavy-handedness towards the opposition. (OMRI)

Members of the Socialist Party and Belgrade city authorities took over NTV Studio B, Serbia's only independent television station, on 15 February. In a move reminiscent of the take-over of the independent daily *Borba* in December 1994 (*Index* 1/1995), the Belgrade Economic Court annulled Studio B's registration as a joint-stock company, enabling the Municipal Assembly to secure the founding rights to the station. The takeover has met with strong condemnation from international human rights groups and from the European Commission. (IFJ, CPJ)

Kosovo: Astrit Saliu from the journal *Koha* was arrested on 16 December, taken to the police station and beaten up. Next day he was handed over to Serbian state security officials who interrogated him about a long list of matters relating to political developments in Kosovo and

Koha's stance on them. (SWB)

It was reported on 4 February that President Milosevic has agreed to the setting up of a United States Information Office in Kosovo following a meeting with US secretary of state Warren Christopher. Christopher also reportedly set preconditions for the acceptance of the rump Yugoslavia into the international community including respect for the human rights of the Albanian majority in Kosovo. (OMRI)

SLOVAKIA

The Slovak Radio and TV Council attacked Radio Free Europe's Slovak service on 9 January, alleging biased news reporting and saying that, unless it mends its ways, its licence will be withdrawn. The following day the Slovak Syndicate of Journalists issued a statement claiming that the attack on RFE was a veiled attempt to intimidate the independent Slovak media. The pro-government Association of Slovak Journalists, however, 'fully endorsed' the attack on RFE, as did the official news agency TASR. (SWB)

Staff at the private television station VTV were told by management on 19 February to make their news reports 'pro-Slovak' and only allow opposition politicians on air when they intended to make 'constructive and positive' criticism, according to a report in the daily *Sme*. Martin Lengyel, VTV's news editor-in-chief, resigned in protest. (SWB)

SOMALIA

On 18 December a radio station supporting faction leader Ali Mahdi Mohamed in northern Mogadishu broadcast a warning that journalists writing 'unholy propaganda' may either be executed or have their hands cut off in the future. The broadcast came after an Islamic court ordered the closure of the daily newspaper *Qaran*. No indication of what constitutes 'unholy propaganda' was given. (CPJ)

An Islamic court in northern Mogadishu jailed more than 30 singers, musicians and comedians on 8 January for failing to submit their material for prior censorship. Militiamen pounced as the performers entertained a crowd at a former sports ground where the audience were subsequently held for half an hour. (Reuter)

SOUTH KOREA

Lee Eun-jin, a singer with the well-known group Kot Dahji, and Won Yong-ho, of the Minmaek publishing company, were arrested by the Seoul Police Administration on 3 February for editing and distributing a songbook which 'praises' North Korea. The National Security Law provides up to seven years' imprisonment for those who praise, 'encourage', or 'side with' North Korea. (PEN)

SRI LANKA

The president's office announced on 20 December that the government would repeal the censorship laws imposed in 1995. (*Guardian*)

A suicide bomb attack by Liberation Tigers of Tamil Eelam (LTTE) in the business quarter of Colombo on 31 January killed at least 83 people and injured more than 1,200. In the aftermath, police rounded up about 400 'suspects' from the city's lodging houses, most of them Tamils. Increased security in Vavuniya means that anyone leaving Vavuniya for Colombo has to get a pass after being cleared by the police and the army. (Reuter)

Recent publications: *The Human Rights Commission Bill* (AI, December 1995, 7pp); *Under Scrutiny by the Human Rights Committee* (AI, December 1995, 25pp)

SUDAN

The Khartoum daily *Akir Khaber* was forced to close on 18 January after the National Press and Publication Council revoked its licence. The council said that the paper had published exaggerated articles and incited conflict between Shia and Sunni Muslims which jeopardised state security. The paper had been suspended in July 1995 for two weeks after publishing an article which criticised press laws. (Reuter, RSF)

Voice of Sudan radio reported on 24 January that members of a group called 'Emanating from the Faith' have been arrested for issuing a formal legal directive accusing Hasan al-Turabi, leader of the National Islamic Front, of being an infidel. They accused him of having used a computer to omit or amend part of the Quran. The Egyptian paper *al-Ahram* reported that more than 40 people belonging to the group have been detained as 'outlaws' and thrown into 'ghost houses' where they are being tortured. (SWB)

Recent publication: *The Human Rights Situation in Sudan, July-December 1995* (Sudan Human Rights Organisation, 1996, 22pp)

SWAZILAND

During a strike designed to force the government to allow free political activity, on 23 January police arrested Richard Nxumalo, head of the Swaziland Federation of Trade Unions (SFTU), and the secretary-general, Jan Sithole and his assistant Jubulani Nxumalo. The strike went ahead in defiance of a June 1995 order banning all protest marches. Demonstrations by strikers were said to be the largest seen in the country since the suspension of the constitution in 1973. One striker was reported to have been shot dead and there are unconfirmed reports of other casualties. (MISA)

TAIWAN

On 7 February Taiwan relaxed a ban on the presentation of Chinese films and television programmes, previously perceived as Communist propaganda. The move allows for 10 films a year to play in cinemas and for Chinese soap operas to make up 30 per cent of a network's airtime. (*Times*)

REPORTERS SANS FRONTIÈRES

TAJIKISTAN

The body of writer and BBC correspondent Mohyeddin Alempour was found on 13 December on the outskirts of Dushanbe. A government official described the murder as a 'carefully planned terrorist act' intended to derail the Tajik peace talks. The leader of the Tajik opposition delegation at the talks, Haji Akbar Turajonzoda, however, said that 'it is not a political murder but an act of banditry... Alempour had no political rivals.' (PEN, SWB)

TANZANIA

The privately owned Kiswahili-language newspaper *Majira* was banned by the Ministry of Information, Youth and Culture on the island of Zanzibar on 24 January. The paper was accused of publishing 'seditious and malicious' materials against the ruling party. Editor-in-chief Anthony Ngaiza called the ban 'an attempt to cover up on the rising tension between the opposition and the ruling CCM'. *Majira* had published several articles concerning the general discontent with the election results (*Index* 1/1996). On 26 January Salim Said Salim, a freelance journalist who regularly writes for *Majira*, was banned by the ministry from working as a journalist on the island. It is unclear what authority, if any, the ministry has to make such an order. Charges against the paper's former editor and publishers, however, were dropped on 2 February owing to a lack of evidence. (MISA)

TUNISIA

Press freedom organisations at the UNESCO conference on independent Arab media, held in Sana'a, Yemen, in January, sent an open letter to the Tunisian government protesting that two Tunisian journalists, Kamel Labidi and Sihem Bensidrine, had been prevented from attending the conference because their passports had been withheld.

Labidi is Tunis correspondent for French daily *La Croix-L'Evenement* and Bensidrine is director of weekly *al-Mawqif*, now closed after several government suspension orders. (RSF)

TURKEY

On 22 December Ayse Zarakolu, director of the Belge Publishing House, was sentenced to six months in prison for publishing a book by former DEP chairman Yasar Kaya entitled *The Gündem Writings*. The sentence was later commuted to a fine of TL50,900,000. The same court also sentenced Zarakolu to a fine of TL 1 million for Sadrettin Aydinlik's book *The Dawn of Hard Winter*. On 29 December Zarakolu was fined a further TL42 million for publishing Abdülkadir Konuk's work on assassinated *Özgür Gündem* journalist Ferhat Tepe. All the charges were brought under Article 8 of the Anti-Terror Law ('spreading separatist propaganda'). The same day she was acquitted of charges relating to a book on the Armenian genocide by Vahakn Dadrian (*Index* 4/1995, 6/1995). (*Info-Türk*)

On 9 January Metin Göktepe, journalist for the daily *Evrensel* (Universal), died after being detained during the funeral of two political prisoners beaten to death five days earlier. On 8 January Göktepe had gone to the cemetery to report on the funeral. Police cordoned off the area and carried out hurried burials without allowing religious ceremonies to be performed. Hundreds of

mourners, including relatives of the dead, were detained and taken to Eyüp Sports Centre and to local police stations. Journalists who monitored the detentions and photographed mourners being kicked and beaten by the police were themselves attacked by police officers who seized their films and videocassettes. Several journalists were detained, including Göktepe. He was seen being beaten as he was taken away to Eyüp Sports Centre where he was held for some time. On 9 January, the prosecutor in Eyüp informed *Evrensel* that 'police found Metin Göktepe dead in a tea garden in Eyüp where he had collapsed after having been released'. (AI, Reuter)

On 16 January Hasan Özgün, Diyarbakir representative of the defunct daily *Özgür Gündem* (Free Agenda), was sentenced to 12 years' imprisonment. Özgün, who had been in custody since December 1993, was found guilty under Paragraph 168 of the Penal Code ('being a member of an armed organisation'). (*Özgür Politika*)

Reuter correspondent Aliza Marcus (*Index* 6/1995) had her application for a new press card denied in February, effectively preventing her from working in Turkey. (CPJ)

TURKMENISTAN

Journalists Mukhamed Muradly and Yovshan Annakurban (*Index* 1/1996) were released on 13 January under a general amnesty, together with 18 others convicted with them of

'hooliganism' in connection with an anti-government demonstration in July 1995. (PEN)

UGANDA

Teddy Sseezi-Cheeye, editor of the influential weekly newsletter *Confidential*, was arrested in Kampala on 21 January. He is being held incommunicado in a police station. No official reason has been given for the arrest although, since its launch five years ago, *Confidential* has angered officials with persistent allegations of government corruption. A court had declared Sseezi-Cheeye bankrupt a week before his arrest, after he delayed paying a fine to a Kampala businessman whom he had accused of robbing a bank. (CPJ, Reuter)

Haruna Kanaabi, editor-in-chief of the Islamic weekly *Shariat*, was released from prison on 27 December, after serving four months on remand (*Index* 5/1995, 1/1996). Kanaabi plans to sue the state for illegal arrest and detention and will demand damages. (CPJ)

UKRAINE

The 31 December edition of the current affairs programme *Pislyamova* (Afterword) was abruptly cancelled after the State Committee for TV and Radio received an unspecified 'phone call from on high'. On 3 January President Kuchma's 'first aide', Volodymur Kuznetsov, said that 'the programme was not banned altogether, and only one broadcast was withdrawn'. But he warned that 'in future, such programmes should be less biased, showing more than one person's opinion'. The problem appears to have stemmed from an item on an earlier edition of the programme about the resignation of a group of presidential aides. The incident was widely reported in the press, but the producers of *Pislyamova* received a warning from administration spokesmen that it was 'not desirable for material on this theme to be shown on air'. On 14 February the producers threatened to take the state television network to court to recover lost advertising revenues from the unaired edition. *Pislyamova* is said to be President Kuchma's favourite programme, but the show's presenter, Oleksandr Tkahenko, has said the producers will stop making it until the country gets its first independent television station. (SWB)

UNITED KINGDOM

In December Cambridge University Press decided not to publish a new book on Greek anthropology, following advice from the security services and the Foreign Office that publication could provoke a terrorist attack against CUP staff in Greece. The book, *Fields of Wheat, Rivers of Blood* by Anastasia Karakasidou is an ethnographic study of northern Greece. It contradicts the Greek government's view that there is no Slavo-Macedonian minority in Greece and raises issues that are central to Greece's dispute with the neighbouring former-

Yugoslav republic of Macedonia. Karakasidou has been threatened in the past in connection with her work (*Index* 3/1994). On 2 February two US academics resigned from CUP's anthropology editorial board in protest at the decision not to publish the book. (*Guardian, Washington Post*, Reuter)

On 3 January the British government bowed to pressure from the Saudi regime, the US government and British arms companies when it ordered the deportation of Saudi Arabia's most prominent political dissident, Mohammed al-Mas'ari. Ann Widdecombe, the Home Office minister, said that Mas'ari's activities 'have been complicating our relations with the Saudis' and that there had been 'various representations from people in British business and the Saudis about the situation...on this occasion we have concluded that British interests as a whole do require his removal.' Mas'ari is appealing against the order. (*Guardian, Independent, International Herald Tribune, Financial Times*)

The BBC cancelled a 65-minute documentary on the life and death of publishing tycoon Robert Maxwell a few hours before transmission on 22 January, after an intervention by Sir Nicholas Lyell, the attorney-general. Lyell warned that broadcasting the programme could contravene the Contempt of Court Act while a decision was being made concerning possible fraud charges against Maxwell's son Kevin. (*Guardian*)

On 30 January the work of Robert Crumb, one of the USA's most celebrated cartoonists, was cleared of all charges of obscenity at Uxbridge Crown Court and cleared for sale in the UK. Crumb's *My Troubles with Women* and *Twisted Sisters* had been on sale in the UK since 1990, but in January 1995 a fresh importation of the two works was seized by customs officers who took offence at two frames in the comics which portrayed oral sex. (*Independent, Guardian*)

USA

The Library of Congress in Washington DC has been forced to cut two separate exhibits in response to criticism. The 'Sigmund Freud: Conflict and Culture' exhibition was postponed on 6 December after protests from academics who said that Freud's theories were now widely discredited. And on 19 December the library scrapped 'Back of the Big House: The Cultural Landscape of the Plantation', after complaints from black staff members and officials that the display lacked a proper historical context. (*International Herald Tribune*)

Following his November ban on the book *Why We Will Never Win the War on AIDS*, on 7 January Judge John Sprizzo ordered the author Bryan Ellison to destroy all copies of the book. Ellison claims that the federal government is trying to silence the growing debate about AIDS research that the book documents. The controversy concerns suggestions by some scientists that the government may have blamed the AIDS epidemic on the wrong cause in 1984 and have therefore wasted millions of dollars in research grants chasing the wrong virus and giving dying patients the wrong treatment. (*Presswire*)

On 12 January the US Supreme Court upheld the ban on indecent television programming outside the 10pm to 6am period (*Index* 6/1995). The ruling was seen as encouraging by the Federal Communications Commission and proponents of v-chip technology. The FCC chairman said: 'We think this means that v-chip legislation would be constitutional.' (*Electronic Media, Communications Daily*)

A US district attorney has decided not to prosecute Philip Zimmerman, the author of 'Pretty Good Privacy' (PGP), the encryption software widely used on the Internet. The spread of PGP has angered the government as it makes it practically impossible for intelligence and security forces to intercept an encoded message. (*Independent*)

The last speaker of the Native American language Catawba, Carlos Westez (Red Thunder Cloud), died on 19 January. The only remnants of the language are in a series of songs and chants he recorded in the 1940s and in his dog, which survives him and only understands Catawba commands. (*Independent, Times*)

President Clinton signed the omnibus Telecommunications Act into law on 8 February. The main provisions of the Act are: cable television deregulation for most systems in the next three years; regional phone companies being allowed to compete in the long-distance markets and local phone services being required to open their networks to competitors; expansion of the broadcast spectrum to allow high-definition television and other future digital services; phone companies are free to offer cable services within the markets in which they now offer phone services; television manufacturers are required to install a 'v-chip' to allow parents to block violent or indecent programmes (*Index* 1/96); it is made a criminal offence to knowingly put 'indecent' material on to the Internet so that it could be viewed by a minor (*Index* 1/96). The last two elements have proved extremely contentious. The online decency provision, which has outraged Internet users, was met with an immediate legal challenge on two fronts: the ACLU, the Electronic Frontier

Foundation and other civil liberties groups brought a test case against it on 8 February; and on 9 February Senators Feingold and Leahy introduced a bill to repeal it altogether. (Reuter)

Lawyers for Mumia Abu-Jamal (*Index* 2/1995, 6/1995) filed an appeal against his murder conviction with the Pennsylvania Supreme Court on 9 February. (Reuter)

UZBEKISTAN

Sergei Grebenyuk, a reporter for the Russian news agency Interfax, was found dead in a canal in Tashkent on 8 February. According to the Interior Ministry, the exact cause of death is unknown. (CPJ)

VANUATU

On 22 January the new coalition government threatened to withdraw the residence permit of Mark Neal Jones, publisher of the independent newspaper *Vanuatu Trading Post* (*Index* 3/1995). The paper had attacked the government's 'localisation policy', which is

Fèca
22.10.95

designed to ensure that foreigners do not get jobs ahead of suitably qualified Vanuatu citizens. (SWB)

VIETNAM

At the end of December the state-owned weekly *Thuong Mai* was shut down for 'lack of objectivity' after reporting on an alleged corruption case. A second publication, the *Business Review Weekly* was criticised by the government for reporting on, but not condemning, the illegal use of firecrackers by residents of Nha Trang. (*Far Eastern Economic Review*)

Pham Dao, director of the state owned telecommunications company Vietnam Datacommunications, has confirmed that it will censor the Internet feed to Vietnam to comply with government regulations (*Index* 1/1996). He said that an Internet firewall could be installed which can screen out transmissions from specified senders or news sources. (Telecom World Wire)

Doan Thanh Liem (*Index* 7/1992), a constitutional lawyer serving 12 years in prison for counter-revolutionary propaganda, was released early on 8 February and permitted to emigrate to the United States. (HRW)

ZAMBIA

Conflict between the government and the independent daily the *Post* has escalated in recent months (*Index* 4/1995, 5/1995, 6/1995). Following the publication on 4 December of a lead story which alleged that President Chiluba was born in Zaire to Zairean parents, the paper's offices were stormed by a group of 20 youths from the ruling Movement for Multi-Party Democracy (MMD). They threatened to burn the 4 and 5 December editions of the paper and to block efforts to sell the paper on the streets. The article was published after President Chiluba attempted to have former president Kenneth Kaunda deported for being of Malawian parentage. On 18 December, during an MMD convention, an editor from the *Post*, Masautso Phiri and his wife, were beaten by MMD members who accused Phiri of attempting to destabilise the president. The 5 February edition of the *Post* newspaper was banned to prevent publication of an article detailing a secret government plan to force through a revised constitution. The paper's editor-in-chief, Fred M'membe, managing editor Bright Mwape and Masautso Phiri were arrested and charged under the Official Secrets Act and Possession of Prohibited Publications Act. Charges under the latter statute were later dropped. Despite a government announcement on 15 February that there will be a referendum on the new constitution, the 5 February edition of the *Post* remains banned. On 7 February the ban was extended to the paper's website (http://www.zamnet.zm/zamnet/post/post.html), after a senior police official ordered Zamnet Communications, which hosts the site, to remove the material. (MISA, CPJ)

The managing editor of the state-owned *Times of Zambia*, Arthur Simuchoba (*Index* 6/1995), was dismissed by the paper's board on 19 February. The dismissal has been roundly condemned by opposition politicians and the Zambia Union of Journalists as a political move. Simuchoba is seen as an independent-minded editor, who has published articles highly critical of the government. The board has given no reason for the dismissal. (*Post*)

ZIMBABWE

Following a demonstration organised by the human rights group Zimrights, President Mugabe warned that the government will deal sternly with organisations 'posing as religious or human rights groups'. Mugabe singled out Zimrights as 'one of the elements bent on creating chaos in the country'. The demonstration was held to protest the killing by two police officers of innocent by-standers during an attempted arrest. (MISA, ZBC)

★ ★ ★

Compiled by: Anna Feldman, Lara Pawson, Kate Thal (Africa); Nathalie de Broglio, Dagmar Schlüter, James Solomon (Americas); Nicholas McAulay, Sarah Smith, Saul Venit (Asia); Laura Bruni, Robert Horvath, Robin Jones, Oleg Panfilov, Vera Rich (eastern Europe and CIS); Michaela Becker, Philippa Nugent (Middle East); Jamie McLeish, Predrag Zivkovic (western Europe)

From Salman Rushdie

FOR those of us who cannot imagine a future without books, it is disturbing to note how many present-day visions have no room for books at all. The view from Bill Gates to *Blade Runner* is distinctly post-literate. For those of us who write books, it sometimes seems that it's open season on writers around the world nowadays, a horrifying state of affairs which this indispensable magazine does so much to record and to protest against. And for those of us who are as concerned about the right to read what we choose as the right to write what we choose, it is alarming that the business of demanding bans on whatever ideas get up people's noses is getting to be respectable. It's getting to be *cool*.

Futurology can be defined as the science of being wrong about the future, and novelists are no better at this kind of speculation than anyone else. Bad news being more glamorous than good, dystopic predictions are far easier to come up with than optimistic ones, and have more apparent credibility. Trapped between indifference and persecution, looking increasingly anachronistic beside the new information technology, what chance of survival does literature have? It's easy to shrug despairingly and start preparing the obituaries.

And yet, I find myself wanting to take issue with this facile despair. It is perhaps the low-tech nature of the act of writing that will save it. Means of artistic expression that require large quantities of finance and sophisticated technology — films, plays, records — become, by virtue of that dependence, easy to censor and to control. But what one writer can make in the solitude of one room is something no power can easily destroy.

© Salman Rushdie, 1996

New censors

As the International Publishers Association meets for its 25th Freedom to Publish Congress, *Index* looks at the threats to publishing old and new

Illustrated by Milen Radev

This report was published with the financial support of:

Den Danske Forlæggerforening; Syndicat National de l'Édition, France; Börsenverein des Deutschen Buchhandels e. V; Federación de Gremios de Editores de España; Association of American Publishers

CAMERA PRESS

German publishing 1480

SIGMUND STRØMME

An eternal battlefield

SEVEN years ago a message from Tehran shocked the world. The *fatwa* against Salman Rushdie and his associates was a reminder that freedom to publish is essential if other fundamental freedoms — the writer's right to write and the reader's right to read — are to be implemented. These are the invisible pillars of democracy, a process that assumes free elections by well-informed voters.

Paradoxically, this correlation, often neglected by western politicians, was never underestimated by totalitarian leaders. The most dramatic manifestation of this bizarre understanding was Hitler's infamous bonfire of books in Berlin in 1933. But the clamp-down on literature was no less efficient under the expanding Communist system. Oleg Grinevskij — Russian ambassador to Sweden with high level experience from the Soviet Union – puts it succinctly: 'There is nothing a totalitarian system fears more than openness.'

As we know, however, even democratic constitutions are not always adequate guarantors of people's right to know. The fear of openness is still evident — though in more subtle form — in the inclination of governments to withhold information from the general public. This often creates tension between state bureaucracy and the media. The secrecy surrounding the arms trade, a subject that is well protected from substantial investigative media coverage, comes into this grey area. While this may be of considerable economic and political importance to governments, it is cold comfort for a soldier on the battlefield to know that he was hit by a grenade produced in his own country.

T HE term 'censorship' is today discredited, its practice no longer publicly admitted. This is a good omen. But it still flourishes in different forms and disguises. One especially strong blend is the combination of political and religious censorship — often linked with suppression and discrimination against ethnic minorities. In addition to the traditional limitations, including military and state security, new threats to the free flow of information include commercial pressures, the secrecy surrounding financial transactions and restrictions on scientific and technological knowledge, all of which pave the way for the most dangerous and morally degrading form of censorship: self-censorship.

The official justifications for these limitations on our universal right to freedom of expression and information appear most honourable: defence of state and religion; safeguards against blasphemy, pornography, defamation and libel. Under the guise of protecting young people, censorship in schools and libraries happens even in democracies. The ensuing political and religious indoctrination serves only to strengthen the seeds of prejudice against foreign cultures.

This particular aspect of free speech and the freedom to publish is one of the most important — and most neglected — areas in public debate on the subject. Publishers, as well as writers, journalists, teachers and parents need to be especially vigilant: textbooks are sometimes the most notorious instance of prolonged cultural colonialism.

E DUCATION is the key to our common future — as also a dictator knows (hence his repeated photo-calls with children). But why do the despots of this world — secular or clerical — so fear a single poem, play or novel that they must silence the writer by imprisonment or death? Except for the perverted instinct that recognises the unique power of literature as a medium of communication, there is no simple explanation. Yet their fear is not unfounded. 'The author is a nonconformist,' said Salvatore Quasimodo in his Nobel Prize lecture in 1957, 'The birth of a new writer is always a threat to the existing cultural order.'

Writers, journalists and, increasingly, publishers have been persecuted by totalitarian regimes of all stripes. With the dramatic changes in the old Soviet Union and in South Africa, however, there has been considerable progress. Since 1990, more than 50 countries have introduced multi-party democratic systems. Behind these — mostly peaceful — revolutions lies a long and often painful process in which intellectuals, writers and publishers have played a part, often at the risk of their lives. Throughout this century, illegal *samizdat* or underground publishing has been of great importance in maintaining the morale and self-respect of a people. Yet these new democracies have a long way to go.

Strict censorship cannot be maintained without terrorism. Algeria, Nigeria, Turkey and Iran are among the bleakest examples of this; International PEN's latest 'Writers in Prison' survey highlights other problem areas: China, Kuwait, Burma, Peru, South Korea, Syria and Vietnam. More than 100 countries are listed. However, in spite of the fact that at least a thousand cases are reported each year, no complete register of imprisonments, disappearances, torture and killing is yet available. A much-needed database network enabling the collation of more extensive and reliable documentation from all parts of the world, is now being set in motion. We need more information about the suppression of information. As US Supreme Court Justice Louis Brandeis said, 'Sunlight is the best disinfectant.'

One of the most important challenges currently facing the international publishing community is the development of a closer professional dialogue with China. China is a long way from meeting the criteria of publishing freedom: writers and publishers are still being arrested and sentenced to prison and execution. But changes are taking place and the move to modernity cannot be stopped. There is ample evidence that the stifling of intellectual life and artistic freedom damages a nation's creativity as well as inhibiting its social and economic development. Scientific progress, for instance, depends on academic freedom as the case of the Soviet biologist TU Lysenko shows. With the support of Stalin and Khrushchev, he dominated and ruined genetic science in the USSR for decades with disastrous consequences for Soviet agriculture and environment.

Complaints against violations of human rights are often rejected as 'western imperialism' — an attack on national culture or interference in internal matters. Western intellectuals who support this cultural relativism often fail to appreciate that it discriminates against people who are denied fundamental and universal individual rights. And whom should we support — the oppressed or the oppressor?

Another important — and not unrelated — challenge we face as publishers is the revival of religious fundamentalism. Religion has a unique power to unite and to divide. The totalitarian nature of religious fundamentalism, coupled with its low threshold of tolerance, frequently exploits religious belief in pursuit of political power. Fundamentalist regimes are usually characterised by a strong patriarchal, anti-feminist attitude that tends to segregate women and deprive them of their right to freedom of expression and information.

Illiteracy, too, is a form of censorship affecting hundreds of millions — not only in developing countries. We find society's losers concentrated in this group: the victims of poverty, illness and overpopulation. In many regions their misery is compounded by the active suppression of information on famine, AIDS and family planning, often with fatal consequences. Literacy is the best contraceptive.

If we are to meet such problems in a constructive way, we must give priority to education, books and reading. The act of reading is in itself a creative process: a mobilisation of inner resources. It adds to our knowledge and influences our opinions. This is what makes it controversial. 'War begins in the minds of men,' said the founding fathers of UNESCO. Most armed conflicts are preceded by propaganda campaigns aimed at inflaming and brainwashing the population. Wherever the state tightens its grip over publishing, press and media, we should treat it as an early warning.

The information superhighway, unsurpassed in speed and quantity, has opened innumerable channels for free speech and debate to people who have never had access to the traditional media. It represents a truly democratic rostrum with a vast potential audience, and this is more than a new, global Speakers' Corner: it represents a truly democratic rostrum with a vast potential audience for information and entertainment. It is early days yet and long-term consequences are difficult to predict, but discussions on traffic regulations and restrictions have already started. The maintenance of quality, values and creativity within the new technological framework raises even more complex questions. However new the technology, it is based on the older skills/culture of writing and reading: it is the content, not the carrier that counts. Publishers clearly have a role as well as responsibilities in the development of the superhighway.

While the frontiers in the fight for freedom to publish will continue to expand, the fundamental principles remain the same. Totalitarian regimes continue to demonstrate that artistic freedom will always be under attack: confronted with geopolitical interests, human rights lose out. Even the UN has been accused of covering up human rights violations by member governments; and its international embargoes that include books and journals are, in so far as they assist totalitarian regimes in denying their citizens access to information from the free world, a self-evident contradiction. Moreover, in parts of Latin America, in accordance with a new provision by which publishers are losing their rights, the World Bank appears to be favouring state control of textbooks. Do we need protection against our protectors?

YET progress has been made on many fronts. The borders of the free world are expanding and we are all beneficiaries of more than one culture. While this may in some respects be a source of conflict, it also creates a platform for future dialogue. There is no true realism without a vision. ❏

Sigmund Strømme is the chairman of the Norwegian publishers JW Cappelens Forlag. He is also chairman of the IPA Freedom to Publish Committee and the Rushdie Defence Committee in Norway

NADINE GORDIMER

The measure of freedom

A Nobel prize-winner charges Africa's writers with creating a literature that will 'feed the consciousness' of their readers

T HE MEASURE of freedom of expression is the measure of a writer's freedom. It's as simple as that. This is as true anywhere else as it is in Africa. Year after year, the graph of that freedom in the world has been published on the back pages of every issue of *Index*, the watchdog journal which records and exposes all forms of censorship, all forms of repressive action against those of us who use the word to seek the truth; about ourselves, about our people, about our societies, about our countries.

Year after year, my own country on our continent, South Africa, was on that list of countries where repression of the spoken and written word, in fact or fiction, was seemingly endless. What a euphoric release to turn to those pages now and find that we are conspicuously missing from entries under the letter 'S'! The level of freedom of expression in South Africa now may be measured by our absence. Gone are the days when, to paraphrase Milan Kundera, police files were our only claim to immortality.

There would be no point in dwelling on the ugly past if it were not for the truth of Milan Kundera's other, much-quoted dictum, 'The struggle of man against power is the struggle of memory against forgetting.' So I remind myself, and you, of the kind of situation in which we writers of fact and fiction in South Africa did our work during the years of apartheid, when racism held the whip over the word.

Perhaps this is the only way we have of ensuring that what happened to freedom of expression shall not be allowed to happen again, resurrect under new motives, find toleration among us for what seems to be the good of other forms of building our new society, until it is too late to realise what we have done. And this vigilance is relevant not only to South Africa but to wherever on our continent freedom of expression has been or is being suppressed; it may be threatened anywhere, among any of us, in the future, for governments rise and fall, ideologies, even the best of them, may justify ends by doubtful means. To coin another dictum, let us guard the right to be politically incorrect, even against the passionate loyalty we naturally feel towards any new order which entrenches our highest hopes and convictions of democracy. That is a vital part of our role as writers in Africa. Let us tell the truth wherever we find it and however unpalatable and unwelcome to authority it may be.

Under apartheid in South Africa there was a Publications Act with 90-plus clauses under which a writer's individual works could be banned; in addition, a ban on a writer for her or his political activity meant that the writer could not publish anything, of whatever nature, not even a fairy tale for children. Many of our books were banned, including the fiction and poetry of exiled writers, Alex La Guma, Lewis Nkosi, Dennis Brutus, Mandlaslanga, and at home the poetry of Don Mattera, a novel by André Brink, and the testimonies of political detainees and prisoners, Ruth First, Albie Sachs, Hugh Lewin and DM Zwelonke. I had the dubious distinction of having more of my books banned than anyone elses. Three novels in a row. An anthology of fiction and poetry by black writers, which I selected and edited, was also banned.

But unlike some of my black comrades, I was privileged not to be harassed, in my person, at home; if a black writer's book was banned, it was assumed that since he or she was articulate that writer must be a security risk in a society where all thoughts and ideas that did not conform to the official ideology, whether in social, political, sexual or religious mores, were subversive. There were raids on these writers' homes, their manuscripts were taken away to be buried in police files, sometimes even their typewriters were confiscated, so that the typeface might be compared with that appearing on revolutionary pamphlets. No manuscript was ever returned, even though the typeface didn't match; the message was: stop writing. Shut up.

Shut up shop as a writer. Of course, that was the message in the banning of our books, too; a message we did not heed. For many reasons, principally the difficulty in finding printers who would risk prosecution, and the prevalence of police spies, we did not succeed in *samizdat* publication — the hand-to-hand distribution of illegally printed or manuscript books. But several small ventures — publishing shacks rather than publishing houses — came into being, started mainly by writers themselves, and these were prepared to publish, and sometimes were, indeed, damned, finding themselves with stocks of books they couldn't continue to sell because these had been axed by bans. But publish they did, whenever they could scrape together the funds to do so, and sometimes they got away with the risk.

One of the first successes was Mbuyseni Oswald Mtshali's poetry collection *Sounds of a Cowhide Drum*, which became something of a bestseller, in terms of what poetry can hope for, with 1,500 copies — an early indication that there was a hunger for writings that came from the roots of a culture, buried by censorship, which the commercialism and craven submission to repressive laws of Establishment publishers such as Macmillan and Longmans would not give the chance to sprout.

Now, our new South African Constitution and Bill of Rights guarantee freedom of expression. From the point of view of legislation, in South Africa writers are free at last. If we African writers and readers gathered here today* may rejoice in that, we have every reason to be deeply concerned about the situation, in other territories of our continent, of freedom of expression and the writers whose means, in their personal and cultural task, it is. I share this platform with my comrade in letters and friend, Wole Soyinka, whose remarkable writings are an illumination of all of Africa, and he comes from an African country where the word is bleeding and he himself is an intermittent fugitive from state repression — intermittent, I say, because he refuses to give up his country for exile, and with irrepressible courage goes back again after each time he has had to flee from persecution for his defence of freedom of expression and/or its collaterals...

If we look farther to the north, what we see keeps the alarm bells ringing in writers' heads.

But who else hears them? Who, in the conferences and forums where the problems of our continent seek solutions in the interchanges of the powerful — who takes heed?

I have yet to hear that the recent Organisation of African Unity (OAU) meeting in Addis Ababa had on the agenda the vicious state repression of journalists in Algeria and, following the near-fatal knife attack on the life of Naguib Mahfouz, the latest atrocity in Egypt: the court edict on a university professor that he divorce his wife because, as the author of a work of secular research into the Koranic texts, he was not a fit husband for a Muslim woman. Yet it should be clear to heads of state that, even if they regard writers' freedom as a matter of little importance, religious fanaticism is not only a threat to freedom of the word, although it strikes there most spectacularly. From there such fanaticism extends — because the word *is* the beginning of everything that regulates the order of human society — to the law in general, and ultimately to the ballot-box and the governance of the state: to misuse of power itself, against democratic values.

It is one of the phenomena of the end of our century that while political oppression has been fiercely fought and fairly widely defeated, an ancient threat, a ghoul, has arisen from the past — religious fanaticism. This time it is not the Inquisition, sending to burn at the stake all who would not embrace the Christian faith, but a cult within Islam which pronounces the death sentence or a *fatwa* on writers and journalists: this is the ultimate suppression of free expression, the end of the word, in death.

And from this follows that, although we are concerned, here, with the writer in Africa, there are no boundaries in this matter of the hounding of writers for reasons of religious intolerance. To quote the English poet, John Donne, 'Send not to ask for whom the bell tolls; it tolls for thee.' When it tolls for Salman Rushdie in England, for Naguib Mahfouz in Egypt, for Taslima Nasrin in exile in Sweden, it tolls for all of us, for we cannot know how religious fanaticism — in one of the many forms in which it is growing — in what country, including our own countries, may rise to threaten freedom of expression and the future of our literature. There are insidious signs everywhere, to which we should be alert.

WHAT is our specific role as writers in Africa?

I have said of my own country, from the point of view of legislation, we writers are free at last, we may write what we like, how we like, when we like.

There are other constraints affecting us; but these belong to the general need all over our continent and may be freely tackled. They belong to the Pan-African determination to create free culture with a dimension for the African intellect and imagination that was not recognised under colonialism. Foremost — it may sound fatuous to have to state this — writers need readers... The fact is that low literacy levels in most African countries mean a small readership even in large populations. And what of semi-literacy? There seem to be no statistics on this level of readership, but I know they would be devastating news for the growth of literature. Writers in Africa don't have enough readers; comic-book literacy does not mean an ability to read a story, poem or novel that has more than a vocabulary that consists largely of grunts and exclamatory syllables.

There are educators who want writers to produce books with a restricted and much simplified vocabulary, in order to encourage a reading culture; we are also asked to allow publishers to prune our existing works in this way, cutting out the 'big words'. I am unrepentantly in the minority, because I refuse to allow this. Not because I am not committed to spreading the enjoyment and love of literature to all; on the contrary, because I believe that you become truly literate, from the state of semi-literacy, in quite another way: by learning the 'big words' from interest in the context, the repetition with which they come up as you go on reading. The crucial thing is that the book itself should be so interesting that you can't put it down, even if you miss a word or phrase here or there. And books simplified to routine phrasing, words and constructions worn thin by overuse, will not produce this passion to turn the next page.

Now comes the crunch. Books must be easily available. And free. The vast majority of our people cannot afford to buy books. We do not have enough libraries in Africa; so, in the end, we writers write for the people in cities, who have such access. And even in cities and towns, libraries tend still to be concentrated in what were the old white areas. We have poor libraries in our schools — sometimes nothing more than a dusty shelf of how-to-do-it books and study guides. All this makes our literature elitist.

Then there is the old, much-wrangled-over question of language. It is easy for others to dismiss our continent as a Tower of Babel. Admittedly, even in our individual countries, there tends to be a formidable number of languages from the point of view of writing and publishing for a readership.

And then there is the matter of the European languages acquired from, assimilated from, the colonial regimes. I use the term 'assimilated' because I believe that, in one way, Africa made a tool out of the very bludgeon, the knobkerrie, that was used to knock aside Africa's own languages (which never ever were out for the count, by the way). Africans appropriated European languages, this basic aspect of European culture, while Europeans voluntarily deprived themselves of the chance to appropriate the basic African culture — African languages.

Many of Africa's best writers write in English or another language of the colonial era, and have entered world literature by this path. And no-one could suggest that they should abandon the language they have made their own and use so well. But there is no obvious reason why equally outstanding writers using African-languages should not be translated into European languages, just as writers in Chinese, Bengali, Japanese etc, are translated into English, French or German etc. There is every reason why African language writers should emerge in this way. But first and foremost, as with all writers everywhere, they need to be read at home among our own people. On our continent there is not enough opportunity for writers to develop their talent in their mother tongues, and get published. In many African countries we are told by publishers (countries with Arabic-speaking majorities are the exception) that there is not a large enough public of competent readers to support publishing in African languages: we are confronted, once again, with the problem of illiteracy and semi-literacy.

I believe this is a dead-end, defeatist point of view. Publishing in African languages is a natural component of literacy programmes. I am convinced that there is a vast potential reading public out there which cannot read English, French or Portuguese well enough to enjoy in these languages a novel relating to their own lives, a biography of one of their own heroes, a poem expressing their own emotions. Given the opportunity to read these in an African language they will discover the joys of literature, that life-long pleasure and intellectual stimulation that does not depend on any electronic device, any mechanical equipment, to be operative. I speak broadly of '*an* African language' because in my own country, for example, most black people are fluent in at least two, even three, African languages other than their own specific mother tongue, so that if a writer writes in one of the major languages his or her publisher could be confident in reaching a readership far beyond the mother tongue of the author. What is needed is a system of state subsidies to publishing houses for the publication of works in African languages, with emphasis on good popular fiction, non-fiction and poetry — keeping well away from tracts and the old staples of the school set-work category. Let there be detective stories — heaven knows, Africans everywhere have had enough experiences with the police — and humour; let writers be freed to use the lyricism of the individual tongue to transform the stories of the past and the community dramas and personal intrigues of the present. Let the writer's imagination take off in the words the writer knows from the heart as well as the brain.

The great critic and writer, Walter Benjamin, of the anti-Nazi left in Germany, wrote: 'One of the foremost tasks of art has always been the creation of a demand which could be fully satisfied only later.' If you think about that, it defines the task of the writer in Africa, now; it is surely our task to create a true African literature by giving our people the opportunity to read, and, as an inevitable consequence, to demand of us writings that will raise and feed their right to the fullness of the open mind, their consciousness of themselves as making the life and thought of our continent. ❏

Nadine Gordimer *lives in Johannesburg. She was awarded the Nobel Prize for Literature in 1991.* *The above is taken from a speech given at the Zimbabwe Book Fair, July-August 1995 © Nadine Gordimer*

ADEWALE MAJA-PEARCE

What price liberty?

*T*HE *SATANIC VERSES* apart, there is no offical censorship of books in Nigeria, and this despite the authoritarian nature of the current military regime which hasn't hesitated to close down newspaper houses and even judicially murder a writer for asking awkward questions about who gets what from the nation's abundant resources. The reason for this is largely economic. Books are expensive, which means that the majority of the country's publishing houses, estimated at more than 45, concentrate either on school textbooks, or on the vanity of prominent individuals (such as retired army generals) only too anxious to have their life's achievements recorded for posterity. Neither kind of publishing is dependent on distribution networks or retail outlets, which is why there are remarkably few bookshops in the country's main urban centres. The economic facts of Nigerian life, in other words, effectively absolve the government from the necessity of monitoring who is publishing what, always assuming that a government of semi-literates, which is what military rule amounts to, is even capable of understanding the potentially subversive nature of a work of literature.

The last point is not — or not only — a rhetorical flourish: Ken Saro-Wiwa, the murdered writer, lives on in his books, which are currently selling faster than they can be reprinted. Wole Soyinka's latest offering, *Ibadan: The Penkelemes Years*, which was published in 1994, is freely available on the bookstands at the international airport in Lagos, and yet Soyinka, the country's only Nobel laureate, was forced to flee the country after the authorities impounded his passport. The government is even rumoured to have put a price on his head for, amongst other things, calling the president a 'mimic midget' and a 'mental and spiritual dwarf' in any number of interviews he has given the international media since the present incumbent seized power in a bloodless coup two years ago and imprisoned the presumed winner of the annulled elections.

It is important, in this context, that *Ibadan* is not yet another incomprehensible drama or poetry collection by a troublesome professor with a penchant for long words and tortured syntax, but a straighforward, uncluttered indictment of the 'contempt' and 'hubris' of the current regime, in itself a manifestation of the 'political pathology' of Nigeria since independence over three decades ago. It's entirely possible, of course, that the government isn't even aware of a publication which in any case is well beyond the pocket of the average civil servant or university lecturer (to say nothing of the average student), which also means that it will only be purchased by foreigners — on their way out.

It is ironic, of course, that a literature which has already produced a Nobel prize-winner in its 40 years of existence should offer so few publishing opportunities to young hopefuls. Moreover, the London publishing houses which were largely responsible for launching Soyinka & Co in the first place are themselves reluctant to publish books by new authors which they can only sell to a diminishing market abroad; and while it is perfectly true that no nation's literature should (or even can) be determined by the tastes and standards of foreigners, however well-meaning, it is also the case that the emergent writer will usually trade abstruse ideological considerations for the sake of literary ambition.

And why not? The writer merely wants to see their book in print, which is how they know they are a writer. The choice, then, is between the desk drawer and finding the money to pay a local printer. The number of self-published titles by a younger generation of Nigerian novelists and poets has grown geometrically year-on-year over the last decade. As one would expect, many of these books are little more than unreconstructed polemic (even when chopped up into verse) aimed at the forces which have denied them their place in the sun; conversely, the contempt and hubris of those same forces which think nothing of hounding a Novel laureate into exile for being rude about the president on the BBC means at least that these writers are able to exercise their right to self-expression.

Only recently, for instance, I ran into a human rights activist busy distributing copies of his latest poetry collection inside the headquarters of the country's leading civil rights organisation only a few days after two members of staff from that same organisation had been taken into custody, where they currently remain without charge or trail. The poet in question was himself supposed to be on the wanted list, but only because of his political activities. As for his poems, well, who the hell was going to read them anyway?

One final irony: the day after the then military government banned *The Satanic Verses*, hardback copies of Salman Rushdie's novel were being freely sold by touts at the international airport. And — who knows? — their clients might even have included two or three government officials looking for a good read between Lagos and London because even a government of semi-literates needs a few PhDs, who themselves only survive for as long as they refrain from talking a lot of English grammar.

HENRY M CHAKAVA

The laws of literacy

In spite of the lack of state support, Kenya boasts the largest and fastest growing publishing industry in East Africa

A LTHOUGH state censorship manifests itself in many ways in Kenya, it is not the most significant factor denying Kenyans access to books. Kenya's book publishing industry today is confronted by even more pressing problems: poverty, illiteracy, an underdeveloped marketing and distribution infrastructure plus the absence of a book-buying and reading culture. Publishing in Kenya will continue to remain a minority concern until these issues are tackled; and that will depend on a government with the will and insight to remove outdated laws from its statutes, promulgate new ones and guarantee basic human rights.

Thirty years after independence Kenya still has no clear-cut national language policy. As a result, publishers are compelled to publish unprofitably in any of the three language categories — English, Kiswahili, and mother tongues. Nor, despite attempts in these directions, does the country have an information policy, a publishing policy or a book policy. Efforts to set up a National Book Development Council have so far been unsuccessful. There are also many unresolved contradictions affecting the industry, one of which is taxation. It is not surprising, therefore, that while the government has liberalised book imports, the home-grown variety remains in the grip of a state monopoly.

The industry also suffers from acute shortage of capital. Banks will not lend to it because they consider it risky, and are usually unwilling to accept stocks as collateral. Publishers, therefore, tend to restrict their publishing activity to the 'safe' areas — textbooks and revision books — and to shy away from any long-term investment in areas such as fiction, or academic and reference publishing. This results in duplication in certain safe areas and scarcity in the high-risk zone.

Lack of funds also undermines the quality of the product as publishers resort to cheaper materials, and untrained and inexperienced staff. Even more important, are those books that never get published because the publisher has no funds to invest in them.

With the possible exception of printers, shortage of funds affects everyone involved in the book chain. Bookshops, libraries and schools are all starved for cash; authors make very little from writing.

Poverty remains the greatest obstacle to book consumption in Kenya. The country has a per capita GNP of only US$300, one of the lowest in the world. Problems of unemployment, food, health and housing, take priority over everything else. Education is perceived only in terms of paying school fees and most Kenyans have yet to accept books as an integral part of the education process.

Another worrying factor is that nearly 50 per cent of the country is illiterate and only a small percentage of those who can read has any disposable income or is in the habit of buying and reading books. Eighty per cent of Kenya's population lives in rural areas with no access to all weather roads, postal services or electricity. Promoting and distributing books under such conditions is an arduous task indeed.

THE KENYAN government exercises censorship of the print media by statutes. These are included in the constitution, the Penal Code, the Books and Newspapers Act, the Official Secrets Act, the Films, Stage Plays Act and the Defamation Act. Working through the minister responsible, the government can invoke any of these laws to ban a publication. Among the local publications so banned are *Kenya: Return to Reason* by Kenneth Matiba, and the following journals and magazines: *Voice of Africa*, *Beyond*, *Financial Review*, *Development Agenda*, and *Inooro*, a Gikuyu news magazine previously published by the Catholic Diocese of Murang'a.

The list of banned foreign publications numbers around 20, and includes such books as Salman Rushdie's *The Satanic Verses*, *Quotations from Chairman Mao Tse Tung*, William Attwoods's *The Reds and the Blacks* — and periodicals such as *Who Rules Kenya*, *Revolution in Africa, The African Communist*, and *Sauti ya Wananchi* (Voice of the People) to mention only a few. A ban on a periodical would normally affect all past and future issues. Foreign newspapers or magazines containing an unsavoury story about Kenya have been seized at the airport and destroyed or detained for several days.

For a country of Kenya's reputation, this list is modest. However, over

Sex and the Girl Guides

O N 2 JANUARY another book fell to a presidential banning order. *Family Life*, a guide to family planning published by the US Girl Guides, was an unlikely victim. However, according to the president, the book contains information on sex education 'not in keeping with African culture'.

The Catholic Church applauded the decision but the majority were baffled. Interest in a book few were even aware of has become intense, with many Kenyans keen to discover exactly what it is that has so displeased their president.

the last 10 years, there has been a systematic attempt to stifle creativity. Several writers have left the country after being jailed, detained, or harassed, to live and work abroad. These include Ngugi wa Thiong'o (see box), Abdilatif Abdalla, Ali Mazrui, Alamin Mazrui, Maina wa Kinyatti, Micere Mugo, Kimani Gecau, Ngugi wa Mirii and Atieno Odhiambo. Local and foreign journalists have been arrested and/or beaten up in the course of their duty. Publishers' offices have been raided and vandalised, while printers such as Fotoform and Colourprint have had their machines immobilised and materials confiscated and destroyed. Dramatic performances have been denied licences or cancelled without reason. Between 1987 and 1993 the plays affected included *Kilio cha Haki* (A Cry for Justice), *Animal Farm*, *An Enemy of the People*, *Fate of a Cockroach*, *Drumbeats of Kirinyaga* (a musical) and *The Master and the Frauds*. Ironically, *Animal Farm* and *An Enemy of the People* have previously been prescribed for study as secondary school examination texts.

State censorship is rather more subtle. The Kenyan education curriculum is so packed that it does not allow any time for leisure reading. Consequently, students are now graduating from primary and secondary school without adequate exposure to fictional works. Literature as a subject has all but disappeared from the school curriculum. It has been 'integrated' into the English Language syllabus and students are expected to study only one novel and one play for their secondary school examination, a far cry from the wide range of texts this subject used to attract. The level of written and spoken language has fallen dramatically among young people and they are no longer able to express themselves properly.

The Kenya Schools Drama Festival is another case in point. During the 1970s, it featured original work, usually written by the students themselves, which took issue with social problems such as corruption, greed, road carnage, social inequality, cruelty to women and children and other ills in our society. Then, in the 1980s, the government banned what it called 'political plays' from the festival and advised education officers to censor any plays with political messages likely to divide the people. All plays were to project the country in a positive light, promote development and interpret the president's motto of Love, Peace and Unity. Although the festival continues, it has lost much of its creative sparkle and spice.

This creative lethargy in schools can also be seen at universities and within society in general. Universities have been largely politicised, and a majority of their professors absorbed into the state system. Creativity is stifled through curtailment of literary seminars, journals and writers' workshops, and a general lack of facilities or incentives to promote and reward academic excellence. The country has lost its intellectual climate as well as any debate on important issues.

Society at large neither respects nor rewards creative talent; writers rarely feature on national honours lists. There is no scheme by which talent is spotted or nurtured: no support for community recreation centres, theatre groups, libraries and other artistic activities. There are no policies nor laws that could provide a framework for the creation of such institutions in the future. From the local community through to schools and the highest institutions of learning to professional societies and clubs, not enough attention is being given to the arts. As one would expect, a creative environment cannot emerge in a society characterised by fear and silence.

The creation of state publishing institutions represents another subtle form of state censorship. The two state publishers Kenya Literature Bureau and Jomo Kenyatta Foundation are the only ones allowed to publish textbooks for the Kenyan school system. While commercial publishers are not barred from publishing textbooks, even when these are acceptable, they can only be used as supplementary or reference material. With this one stroke, the state not only controls the content of what is taught in schools, but is able to keep commercial publishers sufficiently weak and without the funds to invest in risky areas like fiction. The state's involvement in publishing lowers standards by discouraging competition and enables it to censor commercially published books. ❏

Henry M Chakava is managing director of East African Educational Publishers and a member of the government task force on the press

NEIL BELTON

Many books, few ideas

The market has become the great homogeniser: it determines what is published, reinforces bias and puts culture in a strait-jacket

THERE is no censorship of books in the West.

Even to qualify this statement is to invite ridicule. In less than half a millennium, the quantity and availability of printed books has increased so much that entering a bookshop can give you a kind of vertigo: human thought rears up like a sheer wall, and you have to find a handhold in order to inch your way across it in the hours our culture leaves for reading. At the Frankfurt Book Fair in the late seventeenth century, after the chaos of the Thirty Years War, you would have found a couple of thousand new titles on offer; now, after our century's barbaric European wars, a single Waterstone's bookshop in Britain can offer 140,000 titles under one roof and, at Frankfurt, the rights to at least twice that number must be available for sale (at least in theory — most of them will stay firmly within their national or linguistic boundaries).

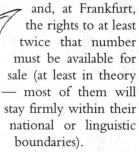

We are right to congratulate ourselves on our cultural good

fortune, and few industries are more prone to indulge that right than the book business. Its calendar has more feast-days than the medieval church, a cycle of dinners and prize-givings at which the same black-clad figures greet each other with the oily sincerity of courtiers in a Webster play. They run companies that can publish anything: formerly taboo subjects and once-invisible preferences explored and marketed with gusto. Writing by in-your-face gays, convivial sadists, furious anarchists, rigorous Marxists, just-about-covert racists; violence by the yard, pornography by the tonne, medicalised advice on every imaginable physical and psychic condition: check out your local bookshop. Classics are available at historically unprecedented low prices, either as full texts or as book-nuggets at 60 pence a bite. It is unthinkable that any point of view can really be suppressed, because books just can't be, and all attempts to ban them have failed; Luther's Bible sold in millions even in the sixteenth century despite the *fatwas* of the Emperor and Pope, and we cherish Rushdie because of the Grand Ayatollah's encyclical. (Or so we like to think: it is one of our most cherished illusions, belied by the industry's refusal to paperback *The Satanic Verses*.)

If the big picture is so nicely lit, why do so many thoughtful people who work in publishing feel concerned about its culture? I think that there are grounds for legitimate doubt about the commitment of the most powerful forces in book production to genuine pluralism and excellence.

The market is dominated by large Anglo-American conglomerates, that also have immense influence on publishing in languages other than English. Books are commodities as well as expressions of imagination and ideas, and the more alike they are the easier they are to sell. Big corporations want as few surprises as possible. This might seem a contradiction in terms if your business is publishing books, but the conglomerates train like athletes for the achievement of predictability.

One of the most insidious pressures in publishing, therefore, is the temptation to think in analogies. This can be helpful as a marketing device (why not call a book 'a Chinese *Hundred Years of Solitude*' if it helps you to sell it?), but in the end it becomes a stiff mould, and it is frightening to watch the jerky manipulation of genres by nervous publishers, a form of cultural auto-eroticism: for example, the legal thriller (fat tomes starring trial lawyers), the thriller of exotic violence (set in a drug-crazed city or the cracker backwoods of the American South, written in a throbbing parody of biblical prose), and, of course, the serial-killer thriller (ad

Battle lines

DESPITE the First Amendment the right to read has become a new cultural and moral battleground in the USA.

Attacks on the Freedom to Learn, a report by the organisation People for the American Way, reveals that 458 attempts were made to remove books from libraries and school curricula during the 1994-95 academic year. Of these, 169 were successful. The state with the highest number of challenges was California (44), followed by Texas (28), Pennsylvania (27), and Oregon (23). The most frequent complaint was that a book's treatment of sexuality was offensive; the next, that it contained profanity. The American Library Association also documents challenges against books in the library system. The book most frequently complained against in 1995 was *I Know Why the Caged Bird Sings* by Maya Angelou, the first volume of her acclaimed autobiography which details her harsh upbringing in the south, her childhood rape and teenage pregnancy. Other challenged books include Mark Twain's *The Adventures of Huckleberry Finn* and *Daddy's Roommate* by Michael Willhoite, a children's book about a child living with her father and his male lover. The most challenged author in 1995 was Judy Blume, whose many stories about the trials of adolescence are clearly deemed too frank for young readers.

The reasons for complaints against books vary. The Christian right object to non-traditional presentations of family life while others protest against portrayals they regard as racist or demeaning. School officials in Georgia, for example, complained that *Huckleberry Finn* 'contains racial slurs and bad grammar and does not reject slavery'. When first published, however, the novel was challenged because it was seen as anti-slavery, a radical view in the nineteenth century. Objections to *I Know Why the Caged Bird Sings* focused on its sexual content; it was 'a lurid tale of sexual perversion', according to a complaint at a Colorado high school in 1994. Members of the Alabama State Textbook Committee claimed that the book preaches 'bitterness and hatred against whites'. Not all challenges are successful, however. Many are defeated by counter-challenges or compromises are reached. One such compromise was reached in Oskaloosa, Kansas, over Katherine Paterson's book *The Bridge to Terabithia*; teachers had to list the different profane words in the book, and their frequency, and forward the list to parents in order to gain written permission for the children to read it. **PN**

Objections 1995

Most challenged titles:

1 *I Know Why the Caged Bird Sings* by Maya Angelou
2 *The Giver* by Lois Lowry
3 *The Adventures of Huckleberry Finn* by Mark Twain
4 *The Chocolate War* by Robert Cormier
5 *Of Mice and Men* by John Steinbeck
6 *Forever* by Judy Blume
7 *Bridge to Terabithia* by Katherine Paterson
8 *Catcher in the Rye* by JD Salinger
9 *More Scary Stories to Tell in the Dark* by Alvin Schwartz

Most challenged authors:

1 Judy Blume
2 Alvin Schwartz
3 Maya Angelou
4 Robert Cormier
5 Lois Lowry
6 RL Stine
7 Toni Morrison
8 Roald Dahl
9 Mark Twain
10 John Steinbeck

Office for Intellectual Freedom, American Library Association

nauseam). This kind of mass production has always been a feature of pulp literature and of pornography, which few publishers now avoid, but it is also true of inspirational business books, new age mysticism, recipe books and celebrity autobiographies.

We all like predictable variation in what we read and in what we listen to, and it is one of the great pleasures of reading trash to discover that the writer is doing it a lot better than he or she needs to, like Raymond Chandler or Elmore Leonard or Sara Paretsky. What is disturbing in the great publishing combines is the emergence of a defiant populism among the executives who run them, for whom 'literary' is a dirty word and publishing commercial genre stuff their only aim in life. The polemic against 'elitism' that accompanies this determination is strange; it is like watching city gents in pinstripe suits stripping to their Y-fronts and dressing up in paint and feathers. It's a deliberate barbarism, like Murdoch's: you can market tits and serial killers, which proves that that is all that people want. Such attitudes are now very widespread, and the hoary old defence of ripping yarns — that they allowed you to publish the really good books — is treated with contempt. Publishing should be driven by the desire to 'make it strange', in a good old modernist phrase. The compulsion to make it familiar is depressing.

This is still a strong tendency rather than a set and hardened attitude in British publishing. But if the market, as any decent economist could have predicted, centralises and homogenises book publishing as well as liberating the trade in ideas, in Britain the domination of a few large companies reinforces quite particular biases in the culture.

Although 'literary' publishing is under pressure, it is still paradoxically true to say that the education of most British editors takes place in a culture that privileges the literary above all else. Books of ideas, of the kind that, for example, address the grand issues facing the republic in America, have to squeeze through a filter woven by FR Leavis, Christopher Ricks or Terry Eagleton. The net is fine, and publishers don't put much energy into encouraging serious work on the agonising dilemmas of British decline. The cultural arteries are further constricted by the narrow base of recruitment of British publishers, chiefly the English faculties of the Universities of Oxford and Cambridge (or the fashionable alternatives like Edinburgh and St Andrews), neither of them exactly laboratories of general intellectuals curious enough to deal with the full range of books worth publishing at the close of the twentieth century.

Another peculiarity of the English is that they don't much like editing books. Historically, British publishers were gentlemen acquirers of authors. The craft-like work on the page that can turn a decent manuscript into something really good, and a powerful but unpublishable text into a book that you will never forget, was done by unsung backroom editors, often women. The conglomerates, usually run by people who have never laid a pencil on a text, don't like editors — all that costly tedious poring over manuscripts — and there are not many of them left. The bringers-in of books are above all that, and far too many books are now not edited at all. Books that would once have been published after being reshaped and coaxed into being by an editor are too much trouble, and are simply rejected. Those who can fit a template of acceptably glib prose get through; the rough and awkward visionary has a harder time of it.

In the West, censorship of books is not the problem. ❏

Neil Belton has published books at Hutchinson and Cape, imprints of Random House. He is now the publishing director of Granta Books

ALBERTO MANGUEL

No minor art

How far are translators 'censoring' their authors' originals?

'We can only prohibit that which we can name.' — GEORGE STEINER

A FEW months ago I finished translating three short stories by the late Marguerite Yourcenar. The stories, published in French under the title *Conte Bleu* which I rendered in English as *A Blue Tale*, are very early works by the writer who was to become, in later life, such an accomplished stylist. Understandably, since they were written with the exuberance and know-all of youth, the stories stray from time to time from sober blue to lurid purple. Since translators, unlike writers, have the possibility of amending the faults of the past, it seemed to me that to preserve every glitter and every volute of Yourcenar's young text would have been nothing but a pedantic undertaking, less intended for lovers of literature than for literary urologists. Furthermore, the English language is less patient with ebulliency than French. And so it was that a few times — mea culpa, mea maxima culpa — I silently clipped an adjective or pruned an outrageous simile.

Vladimir Nabokov, criticised by his friend Edmund Wilson for producing a translation of *Eugene Onegin* 'with warts and all', responded that the translator's business was not to improve or comment on the original, but to give the reader ignorant of one language a text recomposed in all the equivalent words of another. Nabokov apparently believed (but I find it hard to imagine that the master craftsman actually meant this) that languages are 'equivalent' in both sense and sound, and that what is imagined in one language can be re-imagined in another — without an entirely new creation taking place. But the truth is (as every translator finds out at the beginning of the first page) that the phoenix imagined in one language is nothing but a barnyard chicken in another, and to invest that singular fowl (I don't mean the chicken) with the majesty of the bird born from its own ashes, a different language might require the presence of a different creature, plucked from bestiaries that possess their own notions of strangeness. In English, for instance, the word *phoenix* still has a wild, evocative ring; in Spanish, *ave fénix* is part of the bombastic rhetoric inherited from the seventeenth century.

In the early Middle Ages, translation (from the past participle of the Latin *transferre*, 'to transfer') meant conveying the relics of a saint from one place to another. Sometimes these translations were illegal, as when the saintly remains were stolen from one town and carried away for the greater glory of another. This is how the body of St Mark reached Venice from Constantinople, hidden under a cartful of pork which the Turkish guards at Constantinople's gates refused to touch. Carrying away something precious and making it one's own by whatever means possible: this definition of translation serves the act of literary translation as well.

No translation is ever innocent. Every translation implies a reading, a choice both of subject and interpretation, a refusal or suppression of other texts, a redefinition under the terms imposed by the translator who, for the occasion, usurps the title of author. Since a translation cannot be impartial, any more than a reading can be unbiased, the act of translation carries with it a responsibility that extends far beyond the limits of the translated page, not only from language to language but often within the same language, from genre to genre, or from the shelves of one literature to those of another. In this, not all 'translations' are acknowledged as such: when Charles and Mary Lamb turn Shakespeare's plays into prose tales for children, or when Virginia Woolf generously herds Constance Garnett's versions of Turgenev 'into the fold of English Literature', the displacements of the text into the nursery or into the British Library are seldom regarded as 'translations' in the etymological sense. Pork, Lamb or Woolf, every translator disguises the text with another, attractive or detractive meaning.

Were translation a simple act of pure exchange, it would offer no more possibilities for distortion and censorship (or improvement and enlightening) than photocopying or, at most, scriptorium transcription. Alas, *pace* Nabokov, it isn't. If we acknowledge that every translation, simply by transferring the text to another language, space and time, alters it for better or for worse, then we must also acknowledge that every translation — transliteration, retelling, relabelling — adds to the original text a *prêt-à-porter* reading, an implicit commentary. And that is where the censor comes in.

That a translation may hide, distort, subdue or even suppress a text, is a fact tacitly recognised by the reader who accepts it as a 'version' of the original. In the index to John Boswell's ground-breaking book on homosexuality in the Middle Ages, the entry for 'Translation' says 'see Mistranslation' — or what Boswell, in the text, calls 'the deliberate falsification of historical records'. The instances of asepticised translations of Greek and Roman classics are too numerous to mention and range from a change of pronoun which wilfully conceals the sexual identity of a character, to the suppression of an entire text, such as the *Amores* of the Pseudo-Lucian which Thomas Francklin in 1781 deleted from his English translation of the author's works because it included an explicit dialogue among a group of men on whether women or boys were erotically more desirable. 'But as this is a point which, at least in this nation, has been long determined in favour of the ladies, it stands in need of no farther discussion', wrote the censorious Francklin.

Throughout the nineteenth century, the classic Greek and Roman texts were recommended for the moral education of women only when purified in translation. The Reverend JW Burgon made this explicit when, in 1884, from the pulpit of New College, Oxford, he preached against allowing women into the University where they would have to study the texts in the original. 'If she is to compete successfully with men for "honours", you must needs put the classic writers of antiquity unreservedly into her hands — in other words, must introduce her to the obscenities of Greek and Roman literature. Can you seriously intend it? Is it then a part of your programme to defile that lovely spirit with the filth of old-world civilisation, and to acquaint maidens in their flower with a hundred abominable things which women of any age — (and men too, if *that* were possible) — would rather a thousand times be without?'

It is possible to censor not only a word or a line of text through translation, but also an entire culture. Towards the end of the sixteenth century, the Jesuits were authorised by King Philip II, champion of the Counter-Reformation, to follow in the steps of the Franciscans and establish themselves in the jungles of what is now Paraguay. From 1609 to their expulsion from the colonies in 1767, the Jesuits created settlements for the native Guaranís, walled communities called *reducciones* because the men, women and children who inhabited them were 'reduced' to the dogmas of Christian civilisation. The differences between conquered and conquerors were, however, not easily overcome. 'What makes me a pagan in your eyes', said a Guaraní shaman to one of the missionaries, 'is what prevents you from being a Christian in mine.' The Jesuits understood that effective conversion required reciprocity and that understanding the other was the key which would allow them to keep the pagans in what was called, borrowing from the vocabulary of Christian mystic literature, 'concealed captivity'. The first step to understanding the other was learning and translating their language.

A culture is defined by that which it can name; in order to censor, the invading culture must also possess the vocabulary to name those same things. Therefore, translating into the tongue of the conqueror always carries within the act the danger of assimilation or annihilation; translating into the tongue of the conquered, the danger of overpowering or undermining. These inherent conditions of translation extend to all variations of political imbalance. Guaraní (still the language spoken, albeit much altered, by over one million Paraguayans) had been until then an oral language. The Franciscan Fray Luis de Bolaños, whom the natives called 'God's Wizard' because of his gift for languages, compiled the first Guaraní dictionary. His work was continued and perfected by the Jesuit Antonio Ruiz de Montoya who after several years of hard labour gave the completed volume the title of *Thesaurus of the Guaraní Tongue*. In a preface to a history of the Jesuit missions in South America, the Paraguayan novelist Augusto Roa Bastos noted that, in order for the natives to believe in the faith of Christ, they needed, above all, to be able to suspend or revise their ancestral concepts of life and death. Using the Guaranís' own words, and taking advantage of certain coincidences between the Christian and Guaraní religions, the Jesuits re-translated the Guaraní myths so that they would foretell or announce the truth of Christ. The Last-Last-First-Father, Ñamandú, who created His own body and the attributes of that body from the primordial mists, became the Christian God from the Book of Genesis. Tupá, the First Parent, a minor divinity in the Guaraní pantheon, became Adam, the first man. The crossed sticks, *yvyrá yuasá* which in the Guaraní cosmology sustain the earthly realm, became the Holy Cross. And conveniently, since Ñamandú's second act was to create the word, the Jesuits were able to infuse the Bible, translated into Guaraní, with the accepted weight of divine authority.

In translating the Guaraní language into Spanish, the Jesuits attributed to certain terms that denoted acceptable and even commendable social behaviour among the natives, the connotation of that behaviour as perceived in the Catholic Church or at the Spanish court. Guaraní concepts of private honour, of silent acknowledgement when accepting a gift, of a specific as opposed to a generalised knowledge, and of a social response to the mutations of the seasons and of age were translated bluntly and conveniently as 'Pride', 'Ingratitude', 'Ignorance' and 'Instability'. This vocabulary allowed the traveller Martin Dobrizhoffer of Vienna to reflect, 16 years after the expulsion of the Jesuits, in 1783, in his *Geschichte der Abiponer*, on the corrupt nature of the Guaranís: 'Their many virtues, which certainly belong to rational beings, capable of culture and learning, serve as frontispiece to very irregular compositions within the works themselves. They seem like automata in whose making have been joined elements of *pride, ingratitude, ignorance and instability*. From these principal sources flow the brooks of *sloth, drunkenness, insolence and distrust*, with many other disorders which stultify their moral quality.'

In spite of Jesuit claims, the new system of beliefs did not contribute to the happiness of the natives. Writing in 1769, the French explorer Louis Antoine de Bougainville described the Guaraní people in these laconic words: 'These Indians are a sad lot. Always trembling under the stick of a pedantic and stern master, they possess no property and are subjected to a laborious life whose monotony is enough to kill a man with boredom. That is why, when they die, they don't feel any regret in leaving this life.' By the time of the expulsion of the Jesuits from Paraguay, the Spanish chronicler Fernández de Oviedo was able to say of those who had 'civilised' the Guaraní people what a Briton, Calgacus, is reported to have said after the Roman occupation of Britain: 'Thoe men who have perpetuated these acts call these conquered places "peaceful", I feel they are more than peaceful — they are destroyed.'

In our days, censorship in translation takes place under more subtle guises. In certain countries, authors are still submitted to cleansing purges. (The Brazilian Nélida Piñón in Cuba, the decadent Oscar Wilde in Russia, Native American chroniclers in the USA and Canada, the French *enfant terrible* George Bataille in Spain, have all been published recently in truncated versions. And, in spite of all my good intentions, can my version of Yourcenar be called censored?) Often, authors whose politics might be read uncomfortably are simply not translated; authors of a difficult style are either passed over in favour of others more easily accessible or are condemned to weak or clumsy translations; finally (but this may be pushing the notion of censorship too far) authors who write in a vernacular that has no evident correspondence in the translator's language are shackled to explanatory footnotes that condemn them to academia.

Not all translation, however, is corruption and deceit. Sometimes cultures can be rescued through translation, and translators become justified in their laborious and menial pursuits. In January 1976, the American lexicographer Robert Laughlin sunk to his knees in front of the chief magistrate of the town of Zinacantán in southern Mexico and held up a book that had taken Laughlin 14 years to compile: the great Tzotzil dictionary which rendered into English the Mayan language of 120,000 natives of Chiapas, known also as the 'People of the Bat'. Offering the dictionary to the Tzotzil elder, Laughlin said in the language he had so painstakingly recorded: 'If any foreigner comes and says that you are stupid, asinine Indians, please show him this book, show him the 30,000 words of your knowledge, your reasoning.' It should, it must, suffice. ❏

Alberto Manguel is a writer and critic living in Paris. His most recent book is In Another Part of the Forest: The Flamingo Anthology of Gay Literature, *compiled with Craig Stephenson*

ARYEH NEIER

Speaking in tongues

The suppression of minority languages is a recipe for disaster

O N THE EVE of the vote in Quebec on whether to remain a part of Canada, the speaker of the House of Representatives of the United States, Newt Gingrich, suggested that the possible disintegration of his country's neighbour to the north was a warning signal. 'If we don't insist on renewing our civilisation, starting with insisting on English as a common language, we are just going to devour this country,' he said. Gingrich went on to repeat his call to Congress to enact legislation requiring that English should be the only official language of the USA. The effects would be far-reaching, prohibiting practices that range from the printing of ballots and voting instructions in Spanish or Asian languages as well as in English in certain states, to ending bilingual public education in parts of the country with substantial minority populations.

Gingrich's views about the divisive effects of permitting minorities to preserve and develop their own languages are widely shared. On such grounds many governments around the world in states where more than one language is spoken have established an official language and have coupled this with efforts to suppress the languages of minorities. Sometimes this has been a practice of dictatorships, as when Generalissimo Francisco Franco, not long after consolidating power, banned the use of Catalan: or when 'the genius of the Carpathians,' Nicolae Ceauscescu, sought to eliminate the language principally used by Romania's large ethnic-Hungarian minority.

Though the suppression of minority languages is promoted with the claim that it

will have a unifying effect, the actual consequences are quite different. Two notable examples are Sri Lanka and Turkey.

Following independence from Britain in 1948, much discussion in Sri Lanka focused on the dominance by the tenth of the population that had been educated in the English language and spoke it fluently. This produced demands that the civil service and the judicial system should become more broadly accessible through the introduction of the country's indigenous languages. Unfortunately, a segment of the Sinhalese majority and President Bandaranaike pressed a demand for a 'Sinhala-only' policy in the schools and in other public institutions, creating a sharp conflict with the Tamil minority. A country noted for harmonious relations between different ethnic groups became increasingly divided. By now, tens of thousands have been killed and hundreds of thousands have been driven from their homes in a bitter civil war that shows no signs of coming to an end. Though other factors also propelled Sri Lanka's descent into the maelstrom, language policy, and the effort to assert ethnic dominance that it epitomised, did the greatest harm of all.

Turkey also suffers from a protracted internal armed conflict. That conflict has been fuelled by suppression of efforts by its Kurdish minority of about 10 million to use the Kurdish language. As recently as the 1980s, Kurds were imprisoned for speaking Kurdish, or identifying themselves as Kurds ('mountain Turks' was one of the preferred substitutes), possessing tapes of Kurdish music, or giving their children Kurdish names. Today, they have achieved those rights, but still may not form associations along ethnic lines or study in Kurdish in the schools or speak their language on radio and television broadcasts. So far as it is possible to measure public opinion among a minority that suffers from severe repression, it appears that most of the Kurds in Turkey do not seek to establish a separate state. Many Kurds have suffered directly from the more-than-a-decade-long war by the separatist Kurdish Workers' Party (PKK). Yet Turkey's language policy, somewhat modified in recent years under pressure emanating mainly from the institutions of a united Europe in which Turkey seeks its place, has fostered support for the PKK that has helped to sustain its armed struggle.

Though other countries should have learned a lesson from the tragic experiences of Sri Lanka and Turkey, that does not seem to have happened. A small, newly created European country, Macedonia, confronting severe difficulties on a number of fronts, came close to falling apart in early 1995 over language policy.

Macedonia has many ethnic groups — hence, the *salade Macedoine*. The largest minority are the ethnic Albanians who make up nearly a quarter of the population. Macedonia's constitution provides for instruction in the Albanian language at the elementary and secondary school levels, but is silent on the subject of higher education. In the remarkable view of the Macedonian government, this means that university instruction in Albanian is prohibited. When a group of ethnic Albanians attempted to establish an Albanian-language 'university' at Skopje, police were deployed to shut it down. This inspired protests at the scene, and violence broke out in February 1995 in which one ethnic Albanian was killed, several people were injured, and the 'rector' of the university and several other persons imprisoned.

Though the incident at Tetovo did not immediately lead to the escalation of conflict that many feared, the question of higher education remains unresolved. Moreover, tension over language policy could be exacerbated if the Macedonian Parliament adopts the proposal of its speaker, Stojan Andov, to prohibit the use of the Albanian language in its own deliberations. If the proposal is adopted, the Albanian members of Parliament would almost certainly walk out.

Restrictions on the use of minority languages have been adopted by many countries. Far from promoting unity, they are frequently the cause of strife. There are few means of expressing cultural identity that are more significant to minorities worldwide than the use of their own languages. Attempts at suppression often fail, as exemplified by the widespread use today of Catalan in Spain and Hungarian in Romania. Indeed, in the latter case, it should be recalled that the revolution that overthrew the Ceauscescu dictatorship originated among ethnic Hungarians in Timisoara.

It is possible that if Canada had heeded the counsel of some counterpart of Newt Gingrich and attempted to suppress the French language, it could have avoided a referendum that very nearly led to the peaceful separation of Quebec. A more likely scenario, however, is that suppression would have promoted even more intense demands for separation and that the country would have erupted in violence, as has happened in several other parts of the world. ❑

Aryeh Neier is president of the Open Society Institute, New York. Previously, he was executive director of Human Rights Watch

Fortnight

For the last 25 years Fortnight has been the only independent current affairs and arts magazine in the north of Ireland, publishing opinions from all political parties and telling the stories of the north which no-one else does, as no-one else can. Over the last 12 months articles have included:

Jim Gibney (Sinn Féin) on Unionist perceptions
David Adams (U.D.P.) on the state of the union
Robert McLiam Wilson on Seamus Heaney
Robert Fisk on Clinton the peace maker
Danny Morrison on peace in South Africa
Bernadette McAliskey on Sinn Féin
Billy Hutchinson (P.U.P.) on N.Ireland in the year 2000
Fintan O'Toole on President Robinson
Sandy Boyer on Irish America

Yes I'll subscribe to Fortnight:
I enclose a cheque/postal order for £.....................................
Name...
Address..
....Post Code........................
Please send completed subscription form to: Fortnight,
7 Lower Crescent, Belfast BT7 1NR. One-year subscription rates:
UK £24, RoI £28, other Europe £28, US/Overseas £39.
Institutions £10 extra. Students/unwaged £5 discount.   IoC 1

ALEXANDR ZINOVEV

Pawns in a propaganda war

Russian émigré literature was more an arm of the Cold War than a literary venture in its own right

IN THE WAKE of World War II, an unprecedented literary phenomenon broke into the western book market. It embraced the print media, fiction, essays and other texts — all written and printed in Russian. Hundreds of Soviet citizens participated in the creation of these texts. Some wrote them at home and sent them illegally abroad, but the majority emigrated to the West and wrote there. The media, state institutions, cultural and public service organisations, universities, publishing houses, thousands of western journalists, agents of the intelligence services, tourists, diplomats and students — all were involved in the formation and functioning of this 'Russian-language literature in emigration'. Much of it was translated and read by millions and, until recently, held a significant place in western cultural life.

Russian émigré literature was something apart from Russian or Soviet literature. It was unprecedented because it had its roots outside literature, in the Cold War relationship between the West and the Soviet Union. It grew as a result of contributions made by Soviet citizens critical of the Soviet social system, and by western citizens who recognised it as an important weapon in the Cold War. Soviet citizens were encouraged to write, given publicity, material support, the possibility of publication and political asylum. Without western support, Russian émigré literature would never have made a comparable mark on the mid-twentieth-century literary landscape.

My own experience is typical. I had been a critic of Soviet society and Communism since my early youth, and was arrested in 1939 as an anti-Stalinist. But I never intended to formulate my ideas, my experience in a novel or essay. I was sure that it would be impossible to publish such a book in the Soviet Union. I began my first novel (*The Yawning Heights*) in 1974 when Russian émigré literature was already established. If it had not existed, I would not have written the book. Westerners helped to smuggle out the manuscript and find a publisher for it in the West. The book was a success. I was duly expelled from the Soviet Union and became a professional writer — in the West. My book was used by strategists of the Cold War for their own purposes, and I took the opportunity to make public my theory of Communist society.

Russian émigré literature was not a united school. Its participants joined not as a consequence of their literary capacities, education, or taste. They became part of this group as a result of non-literary circumstances: because their aspirations did not correspond to the state of things in the Soviet Union. Western organisations, services, publishing houses and social circles responding to the Cold War gave this heterogeneous rabble a semblance of unity. It was all quite natural. He who pays the piper calls the tune. Every year the German publisher Axel Springer would give the Parisian émigré journal *Kontinent* DM350,000 marks (US$240,000), for example. Kronid Lyubarsky's Munich-based *Strana i mir* received thousands of dollars from the United States; the same is true of Radio Liberty.

Soviet renegades manipulated by western forces became a weapon of western ideology and propaganda. Perhaps not everyone and not in every respect, but this is certainly true of key works of post-war émigré literature. The entire phenomenon was western rather than Soviet or Russian. I set aside its aesthetic aspect (overall I consider it mediocre). Of course, there were creative achievements, but these were exceptions. They remained unnoticed, ignored or underestimated. The media concentrated their attention on the political and ideological aspects of the works in question, as well as the exposure of negative facts about Soviet society. Works which were insignificant from the aesthetic point of view were praised to the skies. Criticism of them was effectively forbidden.

By the early 1990s, the Cold War was over and Soviet Communism defeated. Soviet political leaders performed an ideological volte-face, and thousands of writers and journalists followed their example. Its historical role fulfilled, Russian-language literature in the West collapsed. As a social phenomenon of any significance, it ceased to exist. It was disbanded like a special unit of the western army in the Cold War. Many of its soldiers remained in the West. They continue to write but they are now isolated, unco-ordinated by western forces, splinters of an erstwhile garrison. Several soldiers of the unit returned to Russia, including its general — Alexander Solzhenitsyn. Having lost their former support, prestige and influence, they have sunk into the rubbish heap of contemporary, post-Soviet Russian literature. ❏

Edited extracts from a paper presented at the Igor Hajek Memorial Conference, University of Glasgow, 25 November 1995

Alexandr Zinovev *is a Russian writer and a specialist in mathematical logic. In 1977 he emigrated from the Soviet Union and now lives in Germany. He is the author of* The Yawning Heights *and* Homo Sovieticus

IRENA MARYNIAK

Welcome to the market

Writers in eastern Europe have lost their readers as well as their cosy status under Communism. Publishers, too, are feeling the chill wind of a less than friendly market free-for-all

‘THE PAST is bubbling to the surface,’ says east German playwright Tomas Oberende. ‘There are wounds in the flesh of the victors. The past is with us daily. You can't feel a presentiment of anything, but you can feel post-sentiment.’

For two centuries at least, the intelligentsia of central eastern Europe protected and fostered the languages and traditions that make up the cultural tapestry of the area. Fiercely independent of dogmatic ideologies and workaday politics, intellectuals harboured the region's cultural and moral conscience. In return, they achieved a position within their national communities more socially influential and politically decisive than their academic counterparts in the West could ever hope to enjoy. Where the intelligentsia dictated politics eventually followed.

Since Soviet-style Communism crumbled, the status of authors and artists has plummeted. Their cultural frame of reference has been dismembered and the figure of the successful businessman has usurped the image of the heroic, victimised intellectual in the public imagination.

Now, impoverished, displaced and exposed to the capricious whims of the market, writers must carve themselves a new niche, create a new language and discover new stylistic devices. The days of obligatory metaphor, stylistic subtext, and subtle subversion are well and truly over. *Samizdat* (the Russian term for 'self-published' literature) has been relegated to selected archives. *Tamizdat* (publishing 'out there' in the West) is superfluous, and *tutizdat* (publishing 'right here') is finding its place amid all the production, distribution and marketing traps lying in wait for uncertain newcomers.

The book market has been inundated by profitable, lightweight (often translated) romances and self-help books. Writers have become businessmen, paper prices are rocketing, readers are preoccupied, poor and besieged by alternative demands on their leisure time. Centralised distribution systems have collapsed and, in smaller countries, potential sales aren't significant enough to warrant elaborate marketing operations. Meanwhile, quality literature appears in print runs lower than underground publications once enjoyed. In Hungary, *samizdat* was produced in stencil editions of up to 2,000 copies. Today, publishers won't risk more than a few hundred copies for a new novel. In the 1980s, a Czech émigré publisher could expect to print more copies of poetry and philosophy abroad than he can now, at home. In Poland, *samizdat* editions ran as high as 20,000 copies; the average print run for literature these days is a modest 2,500.

The free market has arrived.

Hungarian blues

UNDER Hungary's comparatively unoppressive Communist regime, any author with the right contacts could expect, in due course, to see publication of a collected edition of his writings. Paper and printing prices were regulated: books could be published for the equivalent of 50 cents. No connection existed between production expenses and sales.

Last year, the challenges facing the Hungarian publishing industry since liberalisation grew increasingly daunting. Production costs rose, the spending power of potential readers decreased. Gross incomes were down by 10 per cent as part of a government austerity programme to control inflation (running at close to 30 per cent). Education and health subsidies fell and daily financial demands sliced away huge proportions of the income of potential book buyers.

'Socialism ended with the introduction of the restriction programme in March 1995,' says Geza Morcsanyi, director of the prestigious publishing house Magveto. 'Paper costs are up and publishing subsidies from the Hungarian Book Foundation and the National Cultural Fund have been cut. The philanthropist George Soros, once the stand-by of quality publishers in central Europe, now views publishing in the region as a black hole and seems to be redirecting funds at education and health care. We are coming close to complete economic *samizdat*. I don't know how we'll survive.'

There are over 1,000 publishers in Hungary (compared to 12 in 1988) but the number is disproportionate for a population of 10 million. Many produce just five to 10 books a year; more serious enterprises will venture 50 titles, offering up a mixture of Freud and cookery, for example. Funders, it seems, have sensed a need to rectify the imbalance created by selective subsidies and are choosing a more cautious line, to allow publishers to find their own space in the market-place. But the sudden change of policy has shaken confidence. Eva Balint of the newspaper *Magyar Hirlap* predicts that only about 200 publishing houses are likely successfully to weather the crisis.

Magveto keeps afloat by attractively packaging a small, select list. 'In the 1960s, books were those little extra gifts piled around the Christmas tree next to the new hi-fi,' Morcsanyi says. 'Now they are prestige items in themselves. The 1980s saw a boom in US style best-sellers like Robert Ludlum and Jackie Collins — all with colourful covers. That's what readers expect.'

Successful translations (including Jostein Gaader, Stephen King, Sigmund Freud and Erich Fromm) have done little for Hungarian authors. Even Peter Nadas, whose books have done well in Germany, cannot now expect to sell more than 5,000 copies to his compatriots. As authors face the prospect of loss of tax allowances for writing, editing and other 'cultural activities', and many seek jobs in the media and elsewhere, the burden on writers is becoming intolerable.

Magveto considers Sandor Tar's *A mi utcank* (Our Street), as the best fictional work of the year, a series of tragi-comic vignettes depicting the rival patrons of two village pubs. The mood is reminiscent of Venedikt Erofeev's *Moscow to the End of the Line* or Bohumil Hrabal's *Closely Observed Trains*. The author is a former factory worker living in an isolated village with writing as his sole source of income. His book has sold barely 1,300 copies.

Tar's absurd, downbeat realism is unusual. According to Gyorgy Bence of the University of Budapest, many younger authors prefer to concoct work out of a melange of inter-war literary tradition and Western post-modernism. 'An unattractive mishmash,' he observes. Publishers are left cold. Much new writing is 'too difficult, negative and esoteric', Morcsanyi says, 'so literary as to be unreadable'.

As young literature closes in on itself and remains largely ignored, print runs fall and publishers collapse, there are signs of deep frustration and anxiety about the future: 'Increasingly fewer and poorer quality books will be produced by fewer staff and authors,' Istvan Bart, chief editor of Corvina Publishers, predicts darkly. 'It is there that the newly won autonomy of intellectual life will come to an end. Publishers will cease to look for books worth publishing. Instead, they will look for works for whose publication sponsors can be found.'

Czech gripes

IN FORMER Czechoslovakia, the fall of Communism triggered a publishing explosion made the more dramatic by the oppression of the previous two decades. The role played by intellectuals in the Prague Spring of 1968 ensured that they were brought to heel by Soviet-installed rulers the following year. Writers and artists were given menial jobs; some were imprisoned or exiled. Cultural life was dominated by a politically acquiescent elite, bolstered by plentiful subsidies donated to ensure wide dissemination of their tightly censored work. The voice of the dissenting few was stifled and confined underground.

When the November 1989 revolution came, there were 36 state or state-approved publishing organisations in the country. By 1991, their estimated number had risen a hundredfold. Initially, former dissidents appeared in print runs of up to 100,000 copies, along with translations of banned western authors such as George Orwell. But interest in the writing of the Czech dissenting intelligentsia waned quickly and the flood of Alistair Macleans followed. Many quality publishers — large and small — went bankrupt. Over the past three years the market has been transformed. Now books on self-development, advice to women, astrology and numerology are all the rage.

'People are interested in how to be successful and keep smiling, *I'm OK, You're OK* kind of books,' says Alexander Tomsky, a former émigré publisher and now managing director of the successful Academia publishing house. 'This is true of Hungary and Poland too; it all follows the same wave. I used to pick things up from the Polish market, which was about six months ahead of us, and publish fast because I knew that good sales in Poland would mean success in the Czech Republic. The differences between central European countries have disappeared as far as the book market is concerned.'

Art, poetry, non-fiction — all 'serious' books likely to command a small circulation — are subsidised by the Ministry of Culture. Most volumes are sold at well below a price allowing for adequate profit margins to make them accessible to impecunious intellectuals. The market is overcrowded, with rising production and distribution costs and, predictably, falling customer spending power. A quality book published in 50,000 copies before 1989 will appear in no more than 2,500 copies today. Sales of the dissident novelist Ivan Klima, which ran into 100,000s in 1990, dropped to 5,000 when he published his latest novel three years on.

'Philosophy or poetry would sell far less,' Tomsky shrugs. 'I try to do print runs of 3,000–5,000, and store them. Then I put the price up as the inflation rate rises and call it a second printing. It's my way of trying to defeat the market. I offer cheaper books and they sell better. But it's a personal strategy and doesn't always work. Sometimes, I transfer the problem into the warehouse.

'Markets of 10 million, such as ours, can barely sustain literature, other than best-sellers. Novels are "out" anyway. But Paul Johnson's *History of the 20th Century* sold 33,000 copies and it's a big, expensive book. Students lap it up because twentieth-century history went ahead without us. We were officially excluded.'

Tomsky's comments on the younger generation of writers are dismissive: 'Communism has left a huge gap between the old masters and people brought up on newspeak. Intelligent and talented the new generation may be; educated they are not. Especially in the formal skills. Their writing is impulsive, spontaneous and amorphous, with disregard for style or form — all highly experimental and often meaningless.'

The sentiment is echoed by the poet Miroslav Holub who complains that if, in the past, a poem had to include at least one Stakhanovite feat, today it must contain an obligatory sex organ or two. 'Culture has lost its communicative powers,' he says, 'Everyone is showing their inner, dark feelings. They are still reacting against the former regime, because it was inadmissible then.'

The self-indulgently gloomy personal world, which seems to be finding its outlines in literature, merges with the discord Tomsky senses in the social landscape: 'Central European societies are atomised and derailed; everyone's busy trying to smile and make a living. People seem to be struggling in isolation against one another and everything around them.

The community has lost its anchor. It's like war. I don't believe that literature can flourish in these conditions. Every household and personality has been similarly destabilised. There just isn't a coherent public to be addressed.'

Polish buzz

UNDER Communism, Poland was in the happy position of having a relatively liberal regime with an immensely influential and confident Church which protected much covert opposition activity, including publishing. After 1977, few attempts were made seriously to suppress an underground press network reaching several million readers.

By the late 1980s the Polish book market fell into three categories: official, unofficial, and 'third circulation' which consisted of a-political underground publications — science fiction, crime and romances — sold at selected bazaars where more risky political literature was generally unavailable. When censorship was abolished in 1989, hundreds of previously underground publishers surfaced to try and make their way in a market of potentially over 30 million readers. Many of these collapsed with just a single book to their credit, but in some cases fortunes were made. Political memoirs like those of the Party First Secretary Edward Gierek or those of General Jaruzelski's press spokesman, Jerzy Urban, appeared in print runs of nearly a million; western spy stories, the *Forsyte Saga* and some previously banned works sold in 100,000s. Prices were low, translators excellently paid. Cheap romances were lapped up, it is said, at a rate of two million a month.

Within three years, however, all major western best-sellers had appeared and sales dropped in a more competitive market. Print runs of commercial literature fell and interest in more ambitious reading matter increased. New writing and poetry were again in demand. Average print runs have now levelled out to around 10,000 copies for books which would once have appeared in editions 10 times the size. New fiction is published in 2,000–3,000 copies with an average selling price of US$5-6.

Beata Chmiel, editor of the literary supplement *Ex Libris,* is confident. Serious reading is back on the agenda; the generation of writers nurtured under Communism has fallen off; the young are working. 'New writers are selling well,' she says, 'but the literature of political resistance is dead and authors of the older generation have been deprived of their intellectual tools. We are in the throes of a conflict of mentality.'

Work from newer authors such as Manuela Gretkowska or Andrzej Stasiuk, may appear experimental at home, but is likely to seem tame in the West. It is geared to shock and challenge traditional Polish perspectives: both the nationalist, Catholic vision and the more liberal ideals cherished by the intelligentsia. Politically, however, most young writers take a conservative political posture, emphasising strong values rather than liberalism and tolerance.

'The 1968 generation now in their forties, has more left-wing sensibilities,' Chmiel says. 'The new right tends to be aged 20 or 30. It's a form of self-definition, you can't assert yourself by replicating the behaviour of the previous generation. These are post-Solidarity people, opposed to ill-defined values and the obscurities of the past. It's not aggressive, but they do have a position on political correctness, feminism, nationalism and the Church. They don't believe in excessive criticism of Catholicism: they don't, for example, see any need to speak up for minorities whose liberties are restricted by the Catholic majority.'

The homogenous political sympathies of young writers in Poland reflect an urge to intellectual uniformity characteristic of groupings within the central European intelligentsia, often delineated by generation, religion or politics. Reluctance to enter into discourse and re-draw the boundaries of group identity, or indeed cultural sovereignty, is a feature of life throughout central eastern Europe. The increasing cultural diversity of publishing here, with waves of market enthusiasm as well as market trauma transmitted between countries, is evidence of the vital and painful impact of open communications and commerce on a region which continues, agonisingly, to seek resolutions to its history of fluctuating borders, enforced rule and cultural fragmentation. ❑

For a comprehensive survey of central European publishing before 1995 see Richard Davy, 'Publishing in the Visegrad countries', Timothy Garton Ash (ed) Freedom for Publishing — Publishing for Freedom; the Central and East European Publishing Project (Central European University Press, 1995)

JOIN THE AMERICAN BOOKSELLERS FOUNDATION FOR FREE EXPRESSION

To Support Our Efforts in Defense of the First Amendment and Free Expression

Bookstores have been on the front lines of the battles to insure that the free flow of ideas and information is never interfered with. By supporting ABFFE you help support a dedicated group of the most effective anti-censorship advocates anywhere in the world.

YES, I want to join ABFFE today.

Individual member (minimum $25.)_____

Organization/Company member (minimum $100.)_____

If payment by credit card:

credit card number/exp. date:_____

NAME: _____

ORGANIZATION/COMPANY: _____

ADDRESS: _____

_____

PHONE:_____FAX:_____

Send payment to: ABFFE, 828 S. Broadway, Tarrytown NY 10591
Fax (914) 591-2716; Phone (914) 591-2665x289.

The American Booksellers Foundation for Free Expression is a not-for-profit charitable organization under the U.S. Internal Revenue Code 501(c)(3).

NICOLE POPE

Open to change

Cosmetic surgery on its
repressive laws has done little to
change the face of Turkey's
onslaught on its writers

BANKS of halogen spots and plush wooden fittings in a pink new
Bosphorus-side tribunal have replaced the old dingy courtrooms, but
the essence of the typical scene at Istanbul's State Security Court is still all
too familiar: a writer or publisher, usually surrounded by a small crowd of
supporters, standing in the dock before three judges.

Until the Turkish Parliament revised Article 8 of the anti-terror law at
the end of 1995, the vast majority of writers, publishers, journalists or
intellectuals who fell foul of the law were tried under this infamous Article
which prohibited 'written and oral propaganda...aimed at damaging the
indivisible unity of the state'. The concept of 'intent' introduced in the
revised Article adopted by the Turkish National Assembly, allowed the
courts to free over 100 people. But the Turkish authorities still have a
whole selection of laws they can use to curb dissent. Article 312 of the
Penal Code, which punishes 'provoking enmity and hatred by displaying
racism or regionalism' is now more frequently used. Behind all the legal
jargon hides one of the major remaining taboos in Turkish society — the
Kurdish problem.

Most of the legal procedures — 5,500 suspects were on trial under the
old Article 8 in 1995 according to the daily *Cumhuriyet* (The Republic)
— are handled by the network of 16 State Security Courts, Turkey's most
zealous and conservative institution. As the conflict between governmental
forces and Kurdish guerillas continues to claim victims every day — more

than 18,000 lives have been lost since 1984 — it is easy to see why the powers behind such institutions feel the need to suppress any thought that goes against the current purely militaristic approach to the Kurdish problem. Yet, ruthless as it may be, the suppression of opposing views has not prevented dissenting opinions from reaching the public.

In fact, were writers and intellectuals not actually being intimidated and sent to jail, the legal proceedings against them could almost be described as farcical. If the aim of the Turkish authorities is to prevent those views from being aired, the court cases fail dismally. The trials of 'star suspects', such as Turkey's most famous writer Yaşar Kemal, who appeared several times at the State Security Court in Istanbul in 1995 after the publication of an article on the Kurdish problem in Germany's *Der Spiegel* magazine for which he was later acquitted, attract media coverage both in Turkey and in Europe. They also give these personalities an added opportunity to state their opinions publicly.

The contradictions do not stop here. Inside the courtroom, the atmosphere is often rather relaxed, despite the potentially serious outcome. Nor do the jail sentences stop these 'convicted criminals' from pursuing their careers. Most of their time in prison is spent writing. Turkish sociologist Ismail Besikçi, a prolific writer of books on the Kurdish problem, whose sentences total more than 200 years in prison, has been in and out of jail constantly. He is usually released after serving one sentence only to be confronted immediately by new accusations after the publication of yet another book.

Fikret Başkaya, an economics professor, and writer Haluk Gerger became cell mates at Haymana prison, after being convicted under Article 8 for writing books critical of the current government policies. Far from being silenced by the state action against them, these two authors gave lengthy interviews to journalists — foreign and Turkish — who were allowed to visit them in their jail. Both were released in 1995, and are still writing.

The Kurdish problem is today the focus of the courts' attention, but the limits on freedom of expression predate the conflict. Publishers acknowledge that writers have been under pressure throughout the 72 years of the Turkish republic. Laws that prohibit insulting the state institutions, the military or republican founder Mustafa Kemal Ataturk are also among the legal weapons used by the Turkish state.

The comparatively liberal constitution introduced after the military coup in 1960 ushered in what is now perceived as Turkey's golden era for personal freedom, and for the publishing trade. In the atmosphere of openness of the 1960s, young people were eager to learn and read. According to the figures released by the Publishers' Association, sales of books then averaged 7,000 copies, but these figures plummeted after the 1980 coup and the introduction of the much more repressive constitution which is still in use today. 'Books and weapons were shown side by side on television,' explains Nurhan Kavuzlu, a young member of the association. 'People became suspicious of books.'

Sales figures are slowly increasing — currently at 5,000 copies on average — as the shadow of the coup very slowly begins to lift. But publishing houses, 70 per cent of which were founded in the past 10 years, face financial difficulties due to increased paper costs and limited distribution facilities. Their problems were compounded in 1995 by the adoption of a new copyright law which raised the intellectual property protection period from 10 years to 70 years — thus harmonising the Turkish copyright law with those of western countries — without giving the publishers a transition period to allow them to clear the books already in production. Most publishing firms were affected by this sudden change.

Many Turkish publishers, struggling to survive, are more worried about the financial aspects of their trade than the political implications of legal barriers. The Publishers' Association president, Anil Ant, acknowledges the current political problems but is keen to show that not all is gloom and doom in the trade. 'There are serious obstacles, such as Article 8, that we want to see lifted as soon as possible,' he explains. But Ant stresses that 'there is no direct censorship in Turkey. We are free to publish what we want, we do not have to ask for permission.' He admits, however, that because of Article 8, publishers do exercise a form of self-censorship. 'Obviously if you think a book may send you to jail, you think twice about publishing it,' he says.

Others, such as Unsal Öztürk, who publishes Ismail Besikçi's books, choose to disregard the threat. Fifty-four cases have been opened against 37 of the 81 books issued by his Yurt publishing house.

When the State Security Court ordered the confiscation of a collection of 11 essays entitled *Freedom of Thought* and initiated proceeding against the authors — among them celebrities such as Yaşar Kemal and the up-and-coming novelist Orhan Pamuk — 1,080 writers and intellectuals signed a petition, stating they were joint publishers of the book, and 50,000 other signatures were gathered to support their initiative. The aim was to force the court to start legal action against all of the 'publishers' and clog the system. The tribunal duly obliged and the case is following its course, but even a prosecutor has suggested Article 8 was unconstitutional.

Such actions by writers and intellectuals are part of a growing social consciousness in Turkey. Ignored for years by those not directly touched by it, the conflict that mainly affects southeast Anatolia is now discussed at all levels, in books, in the media as well as business circles.

It is important to note that Article 8 of the anti-terror law, or Article 312 of the Penal Code are not only used against writers or publishers. In fact, anyone expressing an opinion on the Kurdish problem is in danger of being investigated by the courts. Even an establishment figure, such as Sakip Sabanci, the mogul at the head of the Turkey's number two industrial holding, was the subject of a court investigation after he suggested a political solution to the conflict during a trip to Diyarbakir, the regional capital of the southeast, although the prosecutor's office later decided not to press charges. Professor Doğu Ergil, who published in the summer a controversial report on the situation in the southeast, commissioned by the usually conservative Turkish Union of Chambers, faced prosecution. Reuters reporter Aliza Marcus was tried, and acquitted, for a dispatch on villages being burnt, while well-known columnist Ahmet Altan was sentenced for an editorial entitled 'Atakurd' that asked what Turkey might have looked like if the republic's founder, Mustafa Kemal Ataturk, had been a Kurd.

The trials of respectable figures, as well as the very public proceedings against the venerable Yaşar Kemal, the doyen of Turkish literature — 'the most Turkish of Kurdish writers and the most Kurdish of Turkish writers', according to a columnist in the daily *Cumhuriyet* — have in fact contributed to further the debate in the general public. The accused standing in the docks are no longer just intellectuals who might have been perceived as 'suspect' in the eyes of conservative Turks. Public figures normally considered above reproach — often from business circles — are now speaking in ever-increasing numbers against a conflict that not only burdens Turkey's economy, but also causes dangerous rifts in the population and impedes its integration with Europe.

The European Parliament, under heavy pressure from western governments, reluctantly voted in December 1995 in favour of a customs union deal between Turkey and the European Union. But sceptical Euro

MPs, who felt Turkey had not improved its human rights record sufficiently, let it be known that they intended to keep up the pressure.

The decision on customs union could have far-reaching consequences. The political infighting going on in Ankara has taken the shape of a struggle between an old-fashioned political establishment, eager to keep a tight lid on dissension, and a more modernist — although not necessarily democratic in the eyes of the Europeans — younger generation of politicians, keen to open Turkey to the world. The implementation of the customs union, which should firmly anchor Turkey in Europe's orbit, is perceived by many as an important step towards more openness.

The electoral campaign, prior to the general elections held on 24 December 1995, showed conclusively that Turkish society was ready to discuss difficult topics. Widely different views were expressed by the various candidates — from the Kurdish nationalists of the People's Democracy Party (HADEP) to the extreme right of the National Action Party (MHP) — yet there were remarkably few incidents. The press published lengthy reports on the situation in the mainly-Kurdish southeastern provinces.

Paradoxically, while polls showed 72 per cent of Turks wanted customs union with Europe, the Islamic Welfare Party (RP) — who had campaigned against this free trade agreement — won the general elections held on 24 December 1995 by a narrow margin, mainly because of the deep divisions among the centre parties.

The power vacuum that followed has proved to be yet another obstacle to progress. The RP failed to find any partners willing to collaborate, and the two main centre-right parties refused to bury their rivalry in a coalition. ANAP has until mid-March to bring its current negotiations with RP to fruition.

Turkish society however, which has learnt to live with the ups and downs of its turbulent political scene, continues to open up. Slowly waking up after the long passivity that followed the 1980 coup, it is becoming more politicised, or at least more interested in the outside world.

The board of directors of the Turkish Publishers' Association — like the country itself — is also seeking to forge durable links with its western counterparts. Despite the overwhelming problems facing them, Turks have not lost hope that tomorrow will be better. ❏

Nicole Pope *is* Le Monde's *correspondent in Turkey*

Of such is reputation made

'DEVIANT' Islamic texts and threats to the country's image abroad are the chief forms of book bans in Malaysia. In July 1995 *Bacaan*, a Malay translation of the Quran by Othman Ali, published in Singapore, was banned by the government because it was regarded as a 'deviational' Islamic text, that is to say, a rival interpretation deviating from the official, government-approved versions. The author is a leader of the Quranic Society of Malaysia (JAM), which questions the validity of the *hadith* — sayings and deeds of Prophet Mohammed — regarded by most Muslims as central to Islam. He is also an associate of Dr Kassim Ahmad, an anti-*hadith* writer previously imprisoned for his writing whose own book *Hadith — A Re-evaluation* was banned in July 1986. *Bacaan* was banned on the grounds that the Malay translation is not accompanied by the original text in Arabic and this was regarded as leading to potential misinterpretation. The banning is part of an official policy aimed at outlawing 'deviant' Islamic sects. The most recent to be thus proscribed was the Al Arqam movement in 1994.

Under the Printing Presses and Publications Act and Control of Imported Publications Act, the government can ban any publication for a variety of reasons. Actions have been taken against authors and books deemed undesirable by the authorities. In 1982 imported copies of *The Carpetbaggers* by Harold Robbins, *Juliette* by Marquis de Sade and *The Fan Club* by Irving Wallace were confiscated by police because they were 'prejudicial to the public interest'. Salman Rushdie's *The Satanic Verses,* published in 1989, has also been banned.

The poet Cecil Rajendra, who writes on environmental themes, publishes abroad because local publishers fear the consequences of publishing his work. His passport was seized in 1993, preventing him from travelling to Britain for a poetry reading, on the grounds that he was involved in anti-logging campaigning that was damaging the country's reputation. He has since been allowed to travel out of Malaysia. *PN*

ISABEL HILTON

Blind eyes to the pirates of Beijing

In 1995, publishers spent US$1.5 billion putting their books onto CD-Rom. Good news for the hi-tech pirates, but, goes the consensus, the screen will never replace the intimate pleasure of a good book

A S BUSINESS cards go, it was not without charm. 'Your friend', it said, 'Mr Jian.' There was no address or telephone number, but a paging service number promised swift attention from my 'friend'.

Mr Jian is one of a crowd of young men (and women) who can be found, any day of the week, hanging about at one end of a crowded market street in east Beijing known to foreigners as Silk Alley. On any given day, it's thronged with foreigners in search of bargains: silk underwear, cashmere sweaters, down jackets — all products of China's manufacturing boom. But Mr Jian sells none of these. He's in an altogether more lucrative business: it's a trade that costs western companies millions of pounds a year and one that still threatens to bring the burgeoning commercial relationship between China and its western partners to a shuddering crisis: the wholesale piracy of computer software that goes under the general heading of abuse of intellectual-property rights.

Pity the poor trade officials: the China trade is irresistible because of the size of the market and because, as they plausibly argue, if China is transforming itself into an economic powerhouse, better to have it on your side than waging war, economic or otherwise. But the relationship is fraught with difficulties. Human rights — or, more precisely, to what extent trade sanctions should be used to try to restrain China's human

Sex and the publisher

IN THE lead up to the Fourth World Conference on Women held in Beijing in 1995, the US-based group, Human Rights Watch/Asia produced a report on human rights in China. It pointed out that all books published in China come under the control of the Central Propaganda Department and the State Press and Publishing Administration (SPPA) authorities. Although the numbers of books being published makes control and scrutiny increasingly difficult, there is still cause for concern.

In 1989, after the crackdown on the democracy movement, as many as 41 publishing houses were closed down. Large numbers of books also continue to be banned. These include titles such as *Ancient Crime: Report on the Sale of Women*, published in 1989 and banned as 'pornographic'; *Collection on Chinese Women*, ordered to be destroyed in 1990 for 'problems in thinking and content'; *Memorandum on Marriage and Sex in Contemporary China,* banned in

rights abuses — is one problem that never quite goes away. The running consensus on that one, if the attitude of such trade tzars as the European Union's Leon Brittan is any index, is firmly against pressure.

But the problem of intellectual property rights, unlike that of human rights, is both a moral and an economic issue. Here the spectacle of a game played entirely by Beijing's rules has a cost that can be counted, even by those who cannot compute the value of human rights.

Software piracy was one of the main obstacles in the protracted negotiations over the World Trade Organisation and still threatens to impede China's full accession. Negotiations became so fraught that it looked, at the beginning of 1995, as though a US$1 billion trade war was imminent between China and the USA. That was averted only when a deal was struck in February in which China agreed to crack down on piracy. The deal was greeted by US trade officials with cautious relief. Relief because, having gone to the brink, the crisis was averted. Caution because, as one official put it at the time, the key was in implementation. Ten months on, implementation begins to look like a bad joke.

Mr Jian was at the cautious end of the street traders in Beijing. Proffering his card, he said: 'Just call me. I'll come to your house. I have all the latest software. It's too risky on the street.' His fellow traders seem untroubled by the risk. At the slightest signs of interest a stack of CD-

1990 because one of the essays in the book was said to advocate 'attitudes to sexual liberation and freedom'. It is widely rumoured that the Lonely Planet Travel Guide, *China: A Travel Survival Kit,* has also been banned.

The SPPA has enacted a number of regulations that govern the publication of books on sexual knowledge and sexology. A 1988 regulation stipulates that only publishing houses authorised to produce books on science and medicine may publish such books, and academic studies of sexual matters may only be put out by central level or major provincial publishers. Provincial publishers must get approval before publication from the local government organisations and must report the book to the central authorities.

There also seems to be a belief that if the number of copies of a particular book is limited in some way its impact will also remain thus limited. A maximum of 50,000 copies may be printed of any one book, and they can only be distributed through the Xinhua bookstore. Publishers are also instructed to limit the number of such books on their lists each year. ***Urvashi Butalia***

Roms appear from plastic shopping bags: Windows 95, Encarta 96, the current Grolier, any number of games. The only concession to security is to step behind a slim tree trunk. Prices depend on how hard you are prepared to haggle: they start at £10 and go down to £4. Even at the lower end, the traders seem happy with their profit. 'Come back tomorrow,' they say. 'We've got some new ones coming.' 'Do you get any trouble from the police?' I asked. They laughed. 'They come round sometimes,' said one of the traders. 'Sometimes they arrest somebody. They get a fine or perhaps a week in jail.' 'Then what?' 'Then they come back and carry on.'

The traders are the petty end of the operation, unimportant in themselves except as an index of a steady supply. And as their promise of more in the pipeline confirms, all of the 29 illicit factories that have been identified by US trade officials, and which China had promised in February to close, are still in operation. According to the Business Software Alliance, more than 100,000 illicit CD-Roms had been seized in Hong Kong by September 1995, against only 5,000 in 1994. The cost to US manufacturers of the piracy is conservatively estimated at US$1 billion a year.

When the US protests, China responds that the trade is difficult to control. But in December, Chinese authorities raided a shop in the northwestern city of Xian and seized more than 2,000-pirated CDs. They were illicit copies of Bertolucci's *Little Buddha*.

Was this a belated sign of compliance with its own trade obligations? Not exactly. It was a bizarre offshoot of the latest chapter in China's 'liberation' of Tibet, the enforced rejection of the exiled Dalai Lama's candidate for the reincarnation of the Panchen Lama. The film is banned in China because, the Chinese government says, it promotes the idea of Tibetan independence. Is it not curious that a regime that demonstrates such efficiency in snuffing out political dissent is unable to deal with commercial piracy? ❏

Isabel Hilton is a writer and broadcaster. She is currently writing a book on the Panchen Lama

© *Guardian*

INDEX ON CENSORSHIP

The important issues of the day.
Issues that you cannot afford to miss.

Tolerance
The relaunch issue: Umberto Eco, Salman Rushdie, Ronald Dworkin, Stephen Spender, James Fenton, Dubravka Ugresic, Anne Nelson. *(Issue 1-2/1994)*

Liberty
Vaclav Havel on post-Communist life and Noam Chomsky on US foreign policy. Bob Sutcliffe and Isabelle Ligner on immigration. *(Issue 3/1994)*

Media
Christopher Hird, Ted Turner, Clive Hollick and Matthew Hoffman on the concentration of media ownership. *(Issue 4-5/1994)*

Intervention
Humanitarian aid as the latest form of intervention: Alex de Waal in Africa, Jane Regan in Haiti, Julie Flint in Iraq. The turbulent years since the Velvet Revolution: W L Webb, Ivan Klima and Ryszard Kapuscinski. *(Issue 6/1994)*

Gay's the word
From Moscow, gay life under Communism plus new work from Edmund White, Alberto Manguel, Emma Donoghue, and Lionel Blue. *(Issue 1/1995)*

Death penalty
Christopher Hitchens and Caroline Moorehead on its rising popularity. Helena Kennedy, Alan Clark and Gerry Adams look at liberty in the UK. *(Issue 2/1995)*

Rewriting history
The frenzy of revisionism as we approach Year 2000, with Ronald Dworkin and Eduardo Galeano. Nadine Gordimer on multi-party South Africa. *(Issue 3/1995)*

Women
The counteragenda to the Beijing Conference for Women, with Erica Jong and Naila Kabeer. Plus, Martha Gellhorn and Ariel Hidalgo on Cuba. *(Issue 4/1995)*

United Nations
Michael Ignatieff and David Rieff examine the shaky future of the UN. A US update by Anthony Lewis, Nadine Strossen and Andrei Codrescu. *(Issue 5/1995)*

Film
Roman Polanski, John Waters, Kathryn Bigelow, Milos Forman, Arthur C Clarke, Quentin Tarantino, John Sayles, Ken Loach, Costa Gavras. *(Issue 6/1995)*

You're right. I cannot risk missing a single INDEX.

Send me the following issues at £8 each:

- ☐ Issue 1-2/1994
- ☐ Issue 3/1994
- ☐ Issue 4-5/1994
- ☐ Issue 6/1994
- ☐ Issue 1/1995
- ☐ Issue 2/1995
- ☐ Issue 3/1995
- ☐ Issue 4/1995
- ☐ Issue 5/1995
- ☐ Issue 6/1995
- ☐ Any five issues for £35
- ☐ **All ten issues for only £65**

£_____ total. ☐ Cheque ☐ Visa ☐ MC ☐ AmEx ☐ Diners

Name _____

Card no. _____

Non-UK orders: please add £1 per issue for postage.

Expiry _____ Signature _____

INDEX, 33 Islington High Street, London N1 9LH   Tel: 171-278-2313   Fax: 171-278-1878   II9602

URVASHI BUTALIA

Tracing the limits

Sex, religion — but above all maps — are taxing the Indian censor

A T THE RECENT World Book Fair in Delhi, the organisers, the National Book Trust, had to take as many as 30 books off the shelves. With south Asia as its focal theme, the fair attracted a large number of publishers from Pakistan, Bangladesh, Nepal, Sri Lanka and Bhutan. Many of the books that had to be removed were published outside India, and largely in Pakistan or England. Their depiction of India's international borders was unacceptable to the Indian state, and the National Book Trust, being a state-funded body, had little choice but to have them taken off. In some cases, which did not feature maps or borders, the objection was to the content which, it was feared, could lead to negative reactions on the part of 'certain communities'. Better, it was felt, to be safe than sorry.

This kind of thinking has come to inform the world of books in India increasingly since the Rushdie affair. The banning of Rushdie's *The Satanic Verses* (a ban that still remains in place), and the violence that the book's publication called up, mark a kind of watershed in the history of Indian publishing. Certain kinds of books — and it is difficult to identify exactly which these kinds are — have always been banned or proscribed in India, as in every other country. In colonial India, books considered 'unsuitable' for Indians were often 'killed' by the simple stratagem of cutting off funds, and directors of public instruction had the right to decide what could be read and what could not. In independent India, the state retained the right to proscribe things that were considered 'unwritable': one of the first casualties here was Stanley Wolpert's reconstruction of the plot to kill Gandhi (*Nine Hours to Rama*) which was banned at the time it was published, because it presented a fairly sympathetic portrait of Gandhi's killer.

On the whole though, and before the Rushdie affair, India has had a fairly liberal policy vis-à-vis books. At the time the country became independent, its leaders decided to follow a path of self-reliance: foreign industries were asked to leave, and Indian initiative was encouraged and supported. Heavy duties were levied on the import of foreign items. The only things that remained exempt from this were books. Working on the assumption that the flow of knowledge should be free, the Indian state allowed individuals and organisations to import any number of books from outside. Some marginal restrictions — in terms of quantities — were placed on books that were said to have 'no educational value'; but the purpose of these was to prevent the market from being flooded with foreign books.

Fearful of further violence after the *The Satanic Verses*, the Indian government became much more watchful of books. Three areas were singled out for this: maps and international boundaries (which related to the country's security), religion — and by extension, of course, politics — and sex. In other words, security, politics and morality. The Customs and Excise Act, until recently more or less moribund, was suddenly activated, and set to work in a totally arbitrary manner. Under this Act customs officers are empowered to stop import or sale of anything they consider 'harmful'. It was this that led a customs officer in the southern town of Vijaywada to order a local bookseller, Ashok Book Centre, not to stock Rushdie's *The Moor's Last Sigh*. This order was later extended to cover India (although, interestingly, not before the publisher himself had decided to exercise 'voluntary restraint' by removing the book from Bombay where the local right-wing party had objected to it), and has recently been rescinded.

In recent months there have been many other casualties of this arbitrariness. Included in the books that have been held up at customs are Foucault's *The History of Sexuality* (copies of which have previously been freely available), Freud's work on sexuality, a book of Chinese love poems, and even Louisa May Alcott's book *Little Women*, which it is feared, has 'unnatural sex'. A week or so ago a book on Indian painters, printed outside and brought into the country, was stopped by customs, and no reason was given. Speculation has it that this is because there were paintings which showed Hindu gods in the nude. Earlier, copies of the *Encyclopaedia Britannica* were stopped because its pages on India showed unacceptable borders; another casualty is Anais Nin's *Delta of Venus*. And the Oxford University Press (Pakistan) reports that two of their titles have been held up at Indian customs for over a year now.

ALL OVER the world direct state censorship — of the kind we may have seen in the former Soviet Union, or the kind that is still in evidence in China today (where, in 1989, as many as 41 publishing houses were closed down) — is becoming less common. But overt state censorship has been partially replaced by a kind of censorship exercised by different arms of the state, as in India. This is much more difficult to address, especially when it is accompanied by another kind of censorship.

In many places the resurgence of new nationalisms and the search for 'authentic' identity has led to people appointing themselves guardians of the public morality. It is these people who have taken it upon themselves to prevent, either by violence or by political wrangling, the publication of different kinds of literature. Both

state censorship and censorship imposed by fundamentalist groups are used to pressurise people into imposing self-censorship. It is disturbing to note how this has also led to a kind of self-censorship exercised by publishers.

In December 1993, the government of Mauritius placed a ban on *The Rape of Sita*, a novel by a South African/Mauritian writer, Lindsey Collen (*Index* 4&5/1994). The book had barely been three days in the market when a group of people claiming to represent the 'Hindu community' took offence at its title. Sita, the wife of the Hindu god, Rama, symbolises wifeliness and chastity. The suggestion that Sita had actually been raped was apparently unacceptable to the Hindus, and led the self-styled representatives of the community to demand a ban on the book. The author was threatened with rape, violence and harassment. The government capitulated to the demand and banned the book.

When Collen's novel was banned in Mauritius, there was a very real possibility of it being published in India. However, despite their interest, the publishers were also concerned that in India's current political climate, the very title of the book could lead to a violent reaction against it, and perhaps result in having it taken off the shelves. The dilemma then, was whether to publish the book with the original title and hold true to a kind of 'truth' or 'freedom of expression', or to change the title and perhaps ensure that the book would reach its potential readers. Where, in this, did the responsibility of the publisher lie? In upholding freedom of expression (a phrase that in my view cannot be seen in terms of absolutes), or in ensuring the book's, and the publisher's survival? In the event, no easy answers were found and the book was published in the UK. It remains unpublished in India.

Today, India is one of the largest publishing countries in the world. Official figures put the number of titles published at some 22,000 although the actual number is known to be much higher. Theoretically, and in real terms, the country is a democracy and every citizen is guaranteed certain fundamental rights, including freedom of expression. In fact, however, both at the level of the state and that of civil society, different forms of restraint are shrinking the boundaries of the acceptable. Increasingly polarised along ethnic, religious and identity lines, the growing intolerance in civil society has made it difficult for the voices of dissent and difference to survive. It is important to ask the question: if a book showing 'unacceptable' international boundaries is allowed into the country, will that automatically lead to most Indians believing those boundaries to be correct? If a book that deals with sex explicitly is openly available, will it automatically lead to a degeneration of people's morals? Many of the restraints on books, whether exercised by the state, or its citizens, or publishers, are based on this assumption.

The opening up of the Indian economy to foreign capital and the development of global markets and information technologies could be a positive development for free expression. But globalisation has also placed control of the communication industry in the hands of a few large media corporations. They are now the ones to shape and dictate markets and to determine what gets published. In this scenario, the views and ideas of poor, marginalised people, of women and children, have little meaning.

In such a context, where the question of censorship is beginning to seem increasingly complex, and where it is dictated not only by notions of what is suitable or what is not, but also by a fear of reprisals and violence, it is all the more important to hold out for voices of dissent and resistance. The world of publishing can only be enriched by including in it these different voices. It is only if this is allowed to happen that the concept of freedom of expression will begin to have true meaning. ❏

Urvashi Butalia *is a founder of the publishing house Kali for Women, Delhi*

TASLIMA NASRIN

Siberia in my soul

A YEAR has passed and I am one year older, but the new year has brought no promise nor hope of freedom. Exile has no limits: how long shall I spend the life of a stranger in a foreign land? I see no reason to live in hope of tomorrow.

If someone gave me a single wish, I would answer without a thought: I want to go back to my homeland, Bangladesh. So many years have passed since I left my home. So many years since I last looked on her beautiful face. Sometimes I think I'll go crazy. To those who judge me from outside, I should be happy, content. I don't have to worry about food, clothes and shelter like most of the people back home. I don't have to run for my life any more. There is no *fatwa* nor demonstrations against me. And no spontaneous flow of writing in my life any more.

There are so many caring, friendly people around me here. But still I cannot say I am happy. I've been uprooted from the very soil where I was born and grew up to be myself. Europe: 'the land of dreams' for so many. But what am I here? A rootless person in this alien soil, no sense of belonging. Just another plastic plant in a painted pot. No flowers bloom, even the buds wither away long before their time.

Deep in my soul I still have the urge to create, once more to bring forth the flowers. I want to write again. But for the last year I could write nothing but poems. Poems born from the tears and sighs of my depressed soul. I could describe only my cravings to be a bird and fly back to my beloved Bangladesh. I remember how, in winter, birds from cold, distant lands like Siberia would make their long flight to Bangladesh in search of warmth and sunlight. I too was caught in the wintry coldness of imprisonment in my country when the *fatwa* was announced against me, when they put a price on my head. It was Europe that gave me shelter and saved my life. I can never forget its warm generosity.

But still my heart craves to return. To start my life as a writer again in my old familiar surroundings, among my own people. To sit behind my old writing desk, pen in hand once more. Will Bangladesh remain my eternal Siberia? ❑

Taslima Nasrin *is a doctor and writer from Bangladesh. Following death threats against her by Muslim extremists accusing her of blasphemy and 'conspiracy against Islam' and the banning in July 1993 by the Bangladesh authorities of her novel* Lajja *(Shame), she was forced to leave her country*

KARIM ALRAWI

Fiction's freedom

The government and its Islamic opponents join forces to cripple Egyptian publishing

CIVIL society in Egypt is a smokescreen. The rule of a small military elite is the reality. Translating such a terse statement into practical examples is not difficult. For a start there is the constitution that affords the country's citizens an exemplary degree of freedom and protection, but this constitution was suspended shortly after President Mubarak took over unelected from his assassinated predecessor President Sadat. Another example is that government officials state categorically that there is no censorship of published material in Egypt and will refer the inquirer to a number of laws that they say protect the individual's right to free expression. The truth is somewhat different: the state security forces, or more accurately, the secret police, is not bound by any law passed by Parliament and sets its own rules. The first of these is that local publishers and printers are liable for everything they publish. Publishers and printers must submit to state security two copies of every manuscript they are planning to publish. Even so, they and the publications' distributor must bear the brunt of publishing anything that is deemed unsuitable. The entire stock of the publication may be seized without compensation. They also risk prosecution, fines and prison sentences if they have not informed the security services that what they are about to print or distribute may be offensive to the authorities. In other words, by abolishing the office of book censor that existed in the 1970s the authorities have increased the liability of everybody else in the business and forced them to police themselves. It is not unusual for the employees of a printing firm or distributor to be picked up by the police and beaten or otherwise terrorised into acting as informers on their employer or fellow workers.

A slightly more subtle technique is used with Egyptian assistants to foreign journalists, writers and publishers collecting material for articles or books. Every Egyptian working in such a position has to get clearance from state security. They are periodically called in for a 'chat' and asked to reveal information about the kind of material their foreign employer is collecting. They are also given advice as to when to steer him or her away from material deemed too sensitive for publication, or too critical of the regime. Failure to assist state security results in loss of one's permit to work. A strong incentive to co-operation.

The import of books and magazines is strictly monitored through a branch of the state censor's office which in theory does not exist. The offices for the Censor of Foreign Cultural Artefacts is situated close to the American and British embassies in central Cairo. The offices are in an old apartment block with no sign on the door to alert anyone to their existence. You either know it is there or you don't. Specimen copies of all books and magazines are collected from the airport and brought here, where they are read by a reader and a form is filled out advising whether the publication should be allowed in or not. Decisions are taken as to whether pages are to be torn out of magazines and newspapers or whole issues withheld from the news-stand. Even simple romance novels are read for hidden meanings (Egypt File *Index* 1&2/1994).

Alongside this 'official' government censorship there is the unofficial censorship of the illegal militant Islamic groups. They have a much more straightforward method of suppressing what they dislike. In 1991 they shot to death the writer Farag Fouda. In 1994 they stabbed Egypt's Nobel prize-winning author Naguib Mahfouz. Other cases have involved assaults on writers and the destruction of their property. The unofficial censors derive much of their authority to attack writers from the pronouncements of Al-Azhar, Egypt's one-thousand-year-old Islamic University. Over the last 10 years this institution has become a bastion of religious fundamentalism. In the last couple of years Al-Azhar has, seemingly with tacit government approval, taken up the role of cultural censor, claiming for itself the right to condemn dozens of books, plays, television programmes and film scripts. To be denounced by Al-Azhar is tantamount to a suspended death sentence which may be carried out by any one of the militant groups at any time. In such an atmosphere self-censorship is endemic, both a realistic strategy and a reasonable means of survival.

Three cases in particular highlight the way in which official and unofficial censorship act in tandem to suppress freedom of expression in

Egypt. The first was the 1981 banning of a book on linguistics by Dr Louis Awad, a major figure on the country's literary scene. Agitation by fundamentalists, who said the book was offensive to Islam for claiming that the Arabic language was not God-given and unique, led to a court case and the banning of the book by the government. The second was the prosecution in 1991 of the novelist, Alaa Hamid, whose novel, *A Distance in A Man's Mind* was attacked in the press for being offensive to the prophets of Islam. The prosecution instituted by the government led to an eight-year prison sentence which was eventually suspended because of the international outcry and the writer's poor health.

The third case is that of Dr Nasr Abu-Zeid and his wife Dr Ebtihal Younis, both teachers at Cairo University. Dr Abu-Zeid is the author of several learned books on the interpretation of old Islamic texts. His work offers an alternative reading to the one endorsed by the fundamentalists. The result has been that they have tried to stop him teaching. The ruse they used was to accuse him of apostasy and to then use the courts to try and force a separation between him and his wife. Apostasy is not a valid charge in the Egyptian legal system. Nevertheless, the case was brought to court through the use of a legal term, *Hesba*, from the canon of Islamic law. The courts have effectively accepted the use of *Hesba* and have ruled that the Abu-Zeids must be separated. The opinion of his wife as to whether she wishes to remain with her husband or not was considered unimportant by the court. The Abu-Zeids have now left Egypt after receiving several death threats. This case has far-reaching repercussions. It means that the fundamentalists' archaic interpretation of Islamic law is valid in the civil court and that people can be tried for apostasy. The government's willingness not to interfere in the case gives a green light to further attacks on secular and liberal writers.

The fundamentalist stranglehold on education is increasing. Textbooks are vetted for any material that might offend their sensibilities. The government once opposed to schools imposing the veil on girls in the classroom has recently said that it will not interfere with such demonstrations of public devotion. Neither will it oppose the disgraceful acts of child-female genital mutilation common in many parts of Egypt. Such operations can now be carried out in government hospitals. This practice, once called female circumcision, was all but illegal in Egypt for almost 50 years. Though this brutal custom has nothing to do with Islamic tradition it has been embraced by the fundamentalists. They have declared that writing on this issue and others related to women may be construed as morally corrupting. Women's issues can therefore only be treated from a fundamentalist perspective. As for a subject such as AIDS and the rights of religious minorities, these are said to be part of a great western conspiracy to undermine Egypt's Islamic values and are not to be written about except as ways of attacking the corrupting power of the West.

It is difficult to see how there can be an improvement in conditions in the immediate future given the prevailing social ethos. On the contrary, the more the government appears to side with the fundamentalists the more it encourages them to further terrorise the few remaining advocates of free speech. The government's reasons for acquiescing to the militants is simple: corruption is at an all-time high. With members of the regime having pilfered and stolen such vast amounts of the aid money that has flowed into Egypt over the last 20 years, the last thing they can risk is a move towards democracy and fiscal accountability. As long as writers, journalists, publishers and others are being threatened and killed by the militants, the less likely they are to start shouting about more representative government. But, should anybody feel like doing so the government has passed a large battery of laws (see also page 56) that effectively prevents criticising in writing the actions of any government official. ❏

Karim Alrawi is an Egyptian playwright now living in Canada. He was formerly deputy secretary general of the Egyptian Organisation for Human Rights

LYNNE WALSH

Health warnings

Sex education is part of the school curriculum in the UK but attempts to publish teaching material that goes beyond the birds and the bees have had a chequered career

THE recent history of publications on sex education has been fraught with problems. Government bodies have been threatened with punitive action; school governors have vetoed the use of materials with their pupils; government ministers have banned books altogether.

Anyone who has ever worked in the field would testify that everything is potentially sensitive. Sex education materials have to tackle the difficult questions: how do you know if you are ready for first sex? Who will make the first move? How can you say 'no'? Who will provide the contraception? Should you tell anyone?

And if all that were not challenging enough, consider for a moment the use of language and the tone of sex education publications for, say, 14- and 15-year-olds. If you play it safe, and adhere to medical terminology, will you honestly impart information? If you go too far in using contemporary sexual slang, you may well offend someone. Similarly, if the tone of the sex education text is liberal, or non-judgemental, publishers run into trouble with those who espouse the notion that anyone reading such a book would be encouraged to become 'promiscuous' or homosexual. On the other hand, any text which seems to suggest that heterosexuality is 'the norm' — that fewer people

are homosexual — is likely to be condemned on the grounds of homophobia.

Health educators, then, are well aware that materials may well offend someone. By their very nature, such publications deal with the great taboo: sex. And there have been newer challenges. Since the early 1980s, sex education has had to include information about HIV and AIDS.

Faced with the imperative to help prevent the rise in the HIV epidemic (and other sexually transmitted diseases, plus unintended pregnancies), the work of many health educators seemed to acquire a new bravery. Once the US surgeon general Everett Koop had accepted the need for action, the UK government had to grasp the nettle too. Conservative ministers had to accept the reality of sex in Britain, be it straight or gay, within or outside marriage, above the ages of consent or not.

The new climate did not last long. Responses from small but active groups arguing the case for sex only within marriage, stable family life, denial of gay rights etc, came thick and fast. In 1988, a UK government body, the Health Education Authority, charged with preparing several sex education publications, found its authority severely tested.

Controversy number one came in the shape of 'Teaching About HIV and Aids', a pack designed for use in secondary schools. The government's education department expressed serious criticism and the publication went into a lengthy and complicated phase of 'redrafting by committee'.

One complaint was that the work did not exhort teaching staff to highlight the view that the sanctity of marriage was a protection against HIV. Health educators pointed out that safer sex was the key: individuals could indeed protect themselves by having only one, faithful, lifelong partner, but it was their behaviour that offered protection, not the marriage vows. Civil servants indicated in turn that their ministers wished to see proactive endorsements of marriage and family life, warnings against 'promiscuity' and no encouragement of homosexuality. Government advisers to the HEA also demanded that contacts such as the London Gay and Lesbian Switchboard should not appear in the publication.

The then publisher for the HEA, Irene Fekete, recalls one particularly alarming incident. 'We had worked through revision after revision. We had made compromises, clearly, but the material had integrity and was a vital addition to sex education publications. We had run a successful pilot scheme for the original edition and schools were clamouring for it. However, after all this, the HEA's chief executive Dr Spencer Hagard

Irish stew

U NDER the various Censorship of Publication Acts 1929 to 1967 the Ministry of Justice, through the Censorship of Publications Board, has the power to ban the imprint and distribution of books, as well as other publications. The two categories for banning are indecency or obscenity, and information advocating contraception or abortion (abortion is illegal in the Republic). In the former category banning orders apply for 12 years but in the latter they are permanent, covering books such as *Married Love* by Marie Stopes, banned in 1930, and *The Second Sex* by Simone de Beauvoir, banned in 1961. All books banned by the board are listed in a *Register of Prohibited Publications*, which currently runs to 129 pages.

After the referendum of November 1992, when a clear majority voted for the right to information about abortion services abroad, and the passing of the abortion information bill in May 1995, books about contraception and women's health became more freely available. General women's health books, such as *Everywoman's Lifeguide* and *Our Bodies, Ourselves*, removed from public libraries following a complaint in 1991, were allowed back on the shelves in February 1993. In March 1993 the authorities decided that the widely available book *Choices in a Crisis Pregnancy* by Noreen Byrne, which included information about abortion services in Britain, was not illegal.

More recent banning orders mainly apply to pornographic books; the current *Register* reads like the stock inventory of a sleazy bookshop. However, a campaign by Democratic Left TDs ridiculed the board's continued bans on books such as *Marriage for Moderns* by Barbara Cartland and *The Book of Love* by Upton Sinclair, especially since they appear to have been banned on the basis of their titles rather than any familiarity with their content. The new edition of the *Register*, revised and slimmed down to 550 books and 260 periodicals, should be out soon.

Fear of libel actions serves as a constant reminder of the risk of publishing investigative journalism. Brandon Books paid out costs of IR£100,000 to settle a libel case brought after the publication in October 1985 of *My Story* by Joanne Hayes, the woman at the centre of the Kerry babies' case of 1984. The Irish Book Publishers' Association has since made submissions to the Law Reform Commission to end distributors' liability and bring defamation laws into line with European legislation. *PN* ordered me to publish a *revised* edition with the same ISBN as the original publication.'

Supported by the UK Publishers Association, Fekete refused. The new pack was given its own ISBN, and clearly marked 'Revised Edition'. By this time, the press had revealed that the first edition was being pulped on the instructions of the government.

In March 1994, an HEA publication called 'Your Pocket Guide to Sex' was banned by then health minister Dr Brian Mawhinney. He told the media that he found its contents distasteful and 'downright smutty', and he wanted it withdrawn.

Sex education publications have suffered at the hands of censors, but it has been a murky picture and I would suggest there have been elements of self-censorship on the part of heath educators.

Ultimately, however, it was on the orders of the ministry that publications were destroyed. I asked the Department of Health again recently: 'What was the rationale for taking such a serious step as to destroy a book, especially one likely to carry vital information to its target audience of 18- to 24-year-olds?'

'Because the minister thought it was smutty.' ❏

Lynne Walsh is a journalist, writer and broadcaster specialising in sexual health

1896 – 1996

IPA celebrates its 100th Anniversary at its 25th Congress in Barcelona, 22-26 April 1996

An event no publisher should miss!

CARL MORSE

Whitman = death

Notes on the dangers of real life in the modern school textbook

'The attitude of great poetry is to cheer up slaves and horrify despots.'
—WALT WHITMAN

BY THE TIME, in the 1940s, I reached the ninth grade in Skowhegan, Maine, I had already read everything in the literature textbook. Except for one simile — 'a fingernail moon' — from Dorothy Parker. 'But where,' I asked the assistant football coach teaching ninth-grade English, 'is the Walt Whitman?' For there was none in the textbook. No answer. Because the answer was that it was forbidden by Maine state law to teach Walt Whitman in the schools of Maine. And still is so far as I know.

When, in 1994, I came out to my 84-year-old mother — another, earlier product of the schools of Skowhegan, Maine — she first said: 'Well, at least you don't live around me' — and then, 'I just don't know anything about it.' And I said: 'Where could you possibly have learned anything about it? Not from the schools of Skowhegan, Maine, god knows.' And of course not from its newspaper, its radio programmes, its movies, or its God.

I was reminded of the first time I saw an image of a black person. At the age of eight, in 1942 — on the front page of *The Waterville Morning Sentinel*. It was a wire photo of two 'fuzzy-wuzzies from Papua, New Guinea', carrying a stretcher with a wounded US Army doughboy. I loved their hair. And their shirtless bodies. And the bones through their noses. We never saw bones through noses in those days. Or even natural, shirtless bodies. Hollywood shaved theirs. In the 60 years I knew him, I never saw my father without a shirt on, before or after death. I also loved the fact that there was someone — something — anything! — completely different from the people and the town that engulfed me.

I had long since stopped trying to run away. At eight years old, I had come to believe what my mother said — over and over — that as long as I lived under their roof and ate their food, I was their slave. If I disobeyed, or even so much as ventured to 'sass', I would be killed — or at least beaten until her 'arm dropped off at the elbow'. She always promised that if she couldn't do it, my father would.

So I mostly lived outdoors in a thicket and at the library as much as possible. Mrs Marston, the librarian, let me into the 'big people's' library at a very early age. In fact, she let me into the adult book stacks when I was six or seven — where I holed up for hours at a time. There I discovered Fabre, Rafael Sabatini, and Thoreau. And Whitman. All of them lifesavers. For in my village, we were taught to kill anything resembling ants, pirates, or ideas.

We didn't think to kill sex because it was reputed not to exist — despite the fact that my mother never shut up about it. Every second or so, she would begin to rave about someone she knew or heard of who had got knocked up or had got rid of it or needed to be punished until they learned to control themselves. Having herself got knocked up by the football captain in the back seat of a Model-T, she seemed to know just about everything there was worth knowing about it.

She also knew that Judge Brown was in Thomaston State Prison for being a fairy. Having only ancient country sources for vocabulary, my mother knew just two words for homosexuals: *fairy* and *pervert*. These were fully democratic words, applied equally to male and female. 'I think he's a fairy. I think she's a fairy.' 'It wouldn't surprise me if he/she was one of those fairies.'

I was a fairy, of course. And a pervert. But didn't know it. Because no feeling, quality, characteristic, or behaviour I could identify with was ever attributed or ascribed to fairies or perverts — at least not in my presence — and certainly not in *The Waterville Morning Sentinel* or in my ninth-grade literature book. Even — all innocent and unsuspecting — finding Whitman in the stacks at the Skowhegan Town Library didn't clue me in. Whitman didn't use the word *fairy* the way my mother did. Of course, he did something more important. He told me I wasn't crazy after all — about people and animals and plants — and so to a degree did my other discoveries, Fabre and Thoreau and Rafael Sabatini.

Now I had never met anyone remotely as nice as Whitman or Captain Blood, but instantly determined to do so. It made going on possible. So did descriptions of ants working amicably together and helping one another. So did defiance of the state in *Life without Principle.* I adopted all of these forever.

Still, it would be more than 10 years before I made the connection between me and Judge Brown. And that turned out to be a poor connection after all. For Judge Brown was a boy-lover. And all boys — since I was four — had been my loathed and feared tormentors. Indeed, I remained blissfully ignorant of my fairyhood until I was 19, when at Yale I met my first Captain Blood — a tenor — a fairy — and a rotter. But that's another story.

TODAY, in 1995, 50 years after finding no Whitman in my high school literature text, I am interviewed by a major publisher for the job of writing the poetry sections in a major-state-adoption ninth-grade literature text. In the initial interview, I ask: 'Is Whitman gay in this book or not?' The nice lady editor — light-years smarter than Bill Moyers about poetry — but equally sentimental about life and death — says: 'Not in the ninth grade.' I say: 'What grade?' She says: 'Maybe the twelfth. But not before. Definitely not before.' (I use 'lady editor' advisedly. There aren't many left, but I still know one when I see one. They have grammar. They have manners. They have sentiment and character.)

She gives me samples of the prior editions of this wonderfully lucrative (tens of millions of dollars) text programme, each grade now scheduled to be dumbed down by me and other writers to make editions more suitable to today's classroom. The prior editions are actually quite beautifully constructed. And they contain a fair amount of real poetry. Almost all of this is to be cut.

I am reminded of the razing of Penn Station. And of the French textbook in which I was told to shut up and drop both past participle agreement of reflexive verbs *and* the subjunctive. And of the Spanish textbook in which, over my strenuous objections, Cuba did not appear on the endpaper map of the Spanish-speaking world. Not a trace of Cuba. Not even a hole in the ocean. Cuba — the new Atlantis. Not to mention all the biology textbooks in which, over my retching professional corpse, apologias for Creationism were printed at the front; or the sixth-grade history book that featured a full-colour drawing of beaming Indians warmly welcoming benignant white train-passengers to the Old West; or the high-school science text where a close-up photo of the rampant, curving pistils of a tulip blossom got deleted for being 'too suggestive'.

HULTON DEUTSCH

Whitman the man: frontispiece to the first edition of Leaves of Grass, *1855*

I look up Whitman in the twelfth grade. He is not gay. In fact, nobody is gay in any grade.

On the other hand, mysteriously, *everybody* seems to have colour. This is different from the 1940s, when nobody had colour — except Jeanne Crain in *Pinky*. But now even white people seem to have colour — or pretend to. Curious ethical beiges and pinks — in any event, thoroughly unheard-of casts of temperament, inclination, and reaction — as if race — and better yet — class — do not exist. As if ordinary folks automatically and fully empathise with and understand the Other. Unless, of course, they are gay. In which case, like Cuba, the subjunctive, and scientific fact, they don't exist.

At least, not for American schoolchildren

(I am reminded of the Nixon appointment of an ambassador to France who did not speak French. The French ground their teeth and bided their time. The perfect moment for revenge arrived. US planes had to fly *around* France to illegally bomb Libya. Who better than the French to know that people who choose grunts over conjugations always end up resorting to bombs. God knows what was missing from the maps and verb charts in Richard Nixon's textbooks! Or Jeffrey Dahmer's.)

Moreover, nobody in any grade — author *or* character — is a mean drunk. And absolutely nobody has sex. And utterly nobody kills themselves. And categorically nobody resists authority.

Half the poets printed in this textbook were sex-crazed, state-and-cop-hating alkies and crackheads who went insane or poisoned, hanged, and shot themselves and their neighbours out of despair for justice and humanity and the gods and textbooks exactly like these. I decide to write interesting bios for these poets. My bios are too interesting. They are censored. But I am getting ahead of my story.

With warnings from my supervising editor to be 'accurate', I am anyhow assigned the ninth-grade poetry beat. Another writer has already spent two years producing an unpublishable manuscript. I am given three months to do the same work right.

I glance at the proposed Table of Contents. It has 29 poems. It is essentially the same selection that was in my ninth-grade literature textbook in Skowhegan, Maine, half a century ago! A selection guaranteed, like VCRs, to keep the slaves in line. Oh, some of the poets' names and subjects and titles are different; *but they are essentially the same poems!* No-one could possibly find out what poetry is from this selection. There is no Whitman. None. There is no Millay. There is no Housman. Sure enough, Whitman, Millay, and Housman turn up in the higher grades — in selections as sanitary as unused menstrual pads. So does Allen Ginsberg! For twelfth grade, they have found the *only* poem Ginsberg ever wrote without piss, shit, fuck, corruption, and revolution in it.

Other miracles have been accomplished. Something 'pretty' by Anne Sexton has been unearthed. The Emily Dickinson selection could have been written by Oprah Winfrey. They are using Roethke's 'Papa's Waltz' because they think it's a family poem. (Sure, daddy's stoned out of his skull and slaps us around, but he doesn't really mean it, deep down.) Indeed, not one thought-police person on five levels of selection committees has tumbled to the fact that at the end of 'Papa's Waltz', dear old dad takes little sonny to bed and probably fucks the shit out of him. These same guardians of the faith are also immune to the fact that EE Cummings' poem 'In-Just-So-Spring', which they insist on reprinting, is demonstrably about a child molester.

There are other problems. I am asked to write about figures of speech in poems that have no figures of speech — and about rhythm in poems that have no rhythm, sound in poems that have no sound, and drama in poems that have no drama. I am also asked to pretend that passages of prose are poetry. And that a number of certified non-writers are poets. And, oh yes, I mustn't forget to make this 'poetry' accessible, exciting, and relevant to the lives of 14- and 15-year-old kids — these poems with no metaphors, rhythm, sound, drama, sex, pregnancy, money, power, resistance, booze, or suicide.

There is a poem about going to heaven. And one about fog. And one about rain. And one about snow. And one about flowers and snakes and puppies and hope.

So the first thing I do — unbidden — is spend two weeks developing a list of 120 suggested alternates for this selection of 29 poems. I suggest Whitman, Millay, Housman. I suggest poems with figures of speech, rhythm, sound, and drama. I suggest poems on subjects

Not even black people are allowed to be gay. Or brothers. Not James Baldwin. Not Lorraine Hansberry. Not Langston Hughes. Not Essex Hemphill.

in which ninth-graders are interested. I suggest poems on subjects from which people of any age might learn about something as unfamiliar and untalked about as fuzzy-wuzzies were in Skowhegan, Maine, in 1942. Like privacy. Like slavery. Like mendacity.

Eventually, *one* of my suggestions is accepted. My other 119 suggestions are deemed too 'gritty'. Whitman's 'I think I could turn and live with animals' can't be used because it says something less than kind about Christians. (I remain extremely grateful to have found this out.) 'When I heard the learn'd astronomer' is scheduled to be printed right up to the last minute, when it is suddenly replaced by a reeking piece of religioso shit called 'Forgive My Guilt' by Robert Peter Tristram Coffin. This poem actually talks about 'sin'. This is called throwing the mewling, puking infant off the sledge to the slavering right-wing wolves. This is called the revenge of the 1940s. This is called the revenge of the 1540s. This is called the revenge of the newts. Suggested headline for student newspaper: 'Whitman Replaced by Coffin!'

Ah, but they do after all accept one of my suggestions: Essex Hemphill's poem 'American Hero'. They love it. It is by a black person. It is about basketball. It is about bigotry. It is everything a textbook publisher dreams of. It is new and fresh. The canon has been ransacked over and over, and there are simply no more 'clean' poems left to be discovered. All the clean poems have been printed — over and over — by everybody, especially the competition. So here is a real coup — a clean poem nobody else has ever printed. It also happens to be the only clean poem that black, gay, raunchy Essex Hemphill, a principal of the banned movie *Tongues Untied,* ever wrote.

In Hemphill's biography, I cite the full title of his anthology: *Brother to Brother: New Writings by Black Gay Men.* This title — these nine words — are the only words cut from the bio I have written. These words do not appear in the printed book. Not even black people are allowed to be gay. Or brothers. Not James Baldwin. Not Lorraine Hansberry. Not Langston Hughes. Not Essex Hemphill.

On the other hand, the publisher is so excited to have discovered a new black writer that they ask Hemphill for an author's sidebar. He gives them one that will never see the light of day. Unless Hemphill publishes it from the grave. But they've already got what they want: a clean, safe poem by a black person about basketball and bigotry.

According to my editors, I do 'a wonderful job' on this assignment. I am told that I know how to talk to young people. I am told that my writing on this project is so good that it makes people cry. I am told that at least one editor has posted an especially inspiring sample of my writing on their home refrigerator. I will be asked to write for this publisher again.

For better or worse, I did throw all my energies and talents into doing well what I was asked to do. The story of my life. And I can't honestly say I regret being a pimp and pervert for textbook 'poetry'. Indeed, I may in some ways be healthier for having spread my legs. And I'm not about to return to my orthodontist the new set of teeth bought with this blood money. And I was sincerely glad not to be homeless for those few months. And I got to reread, at someone else's expense, the entire canon of American and British poetry. Yet, unforgettable as the yellow pus of ingrown toenails ('a fingernail moon'!), the moral reservations fester and persist.

But no more so than in other departments of life. And I think I managed — against remarkable odds — to insert into this vast Coffin occasional little spasms of enthusiasm for life and for poetry. And I know I succeeded in insinuating a few smelly, jarring bits that got by the nostrils and tympanums of our self-elected keepers. May they forever remain too stupid to recognise them. (I would like here to pay tribute to the nice lady editor, who — game and feisty, but hopelessly swamped by huns and vandals — defended the faith — and Whitman — as well as she could without relinquishing her head or job. Bless her old-fashioned heart.)

My principal insinuation, of course, is Hemphill's poem 'American Hero'. Not only do I not regret getting this ticking bomb past people who otherwise don't deserve the opportunity to lick the smegma from beneath Hemphill's foreskin, but it lets me imagine that some despairing kid will one day be led by this poem to track down Hemphill's gloriously filthy, moral, dangerous, life-giving poems in the stacks of their local library (assuming there is still life and libraries) — there suddenly to discover perhaps, as I did in 1942, from Thoreau and Fabre and Sabatini and Whitman, that Cuba exists, and that not all of this world is just another kiss-ass con game run by power cretins who whipsaw slaves with bread and circuses — but is equally and forever rife with a billion evolving forms of delicious, drunken, stark-naked, bone-pierced fuzzy-wuzzies who not only look and act queer and un-Disney, but also occupy and uphold supremely factual and sublimely sane subjunctive zones. ❏

Carl Morse, poet and playwright, has been an editor for various major publishers and was for a number of years director of publications at The Museum of Modern Art, New York. Get a Grip, London, has just issued Fruit of Your Loins, *a volume of four plays*

HUMAN RIGHTS

CAROLINE MOOREHEAD

Portrait of a year

Once again, as the human rights organisations deliver their annual reports for 1995, they tell a grim tale of abuse, violation and murder

JUST over a year ago, Said Mekbel, editor of the Algerian daily paper *Le Matin*, was shot dead as he was having lunch in a restaurant not far from his office in a suburb of Algiers. This was not the first attack on his life. Nine months earlier, he had barely escaped another killer.

The day after Mekbel's murder, a spokesman announced that protecting journalists was a high priority for the Algerian government. Yet Algeria, in 1995 as in 1994, was the most dangerous place in the world for a journalist, as the annual reports of the Committee to Protect Journalists (CPJ) and Reporters sans Frontières (RSF) show. Twenty-four died — nearly half the number of all journalists reported killed throughout the world last year. Hundreds more were shot at, wounded, terrified and driven to silence in exile, in a country in which as many as 50,000 people are thought to have lost their lives in a little over three years of murderous civil turmoil. There is probably no family left in the country today who has not been touched by a violent death.

While editors and reporters were dying in Algeria, others were killed in Azerbaijan, Burundi, Somalia and Turkey. In Brazil, four journalists on magazines in different parts of the country were murdered, victims, says RSF, of 'local big-shots whom they had dared to criticise'. Though overall numbers of the dead are actually down — around 50 to 60 in 1995, compared to some 70 in 1994 — what journalists fear most today, according to CPJ, more than stepping on a mine or being caught in crossfire, is assassination, deliberate murder to suppress an unwanted story. The International Federation of Journalists warns that worse may be to come: 'violent intimidation of journalists,' it says, has become 'an acceptable form of pressure'.

Though punctuated by episodes of extreme brutality — Bosnia, Chechnya and Kashmir are all prime examples — 1995 has not, however, been an unbroken disaster in the human rights world. After a decade of shirking their responsibilities, there are signs, according to Human Rights Watch's (HRW) authoritative and impressive report for 1996, that the major powers are gradually beginning to recognise that they can no longer afford to ignore violations either at home or in other parts of the world, without attracting loud public condemnation. Commitment may remain patchy, and commercial interests continue to take precedence, but the sheer volume of public clamour, and the carrots and sticks wielded by the human rights world, seem to be having some effect.

What could be causing some of this stirring of public and private conscience, the annual reports appear to suggest, is the increasingly public nature of failure. In the last few years, governments, the United Nations, the peacekeeping forces and political leaders, have all been seen to fail spectacularly — whether over checking the massacres in Bosnia, protecting civilians in Chechnya, curbing summary executions everywhere from Kashmir to Liberia, preventing the indiscriminate sales of kalashnikovs all over southern Africa and the Indian subcontinent, or halting the steady flow of refugees fleeing terror at home. President Clinton's capitulation to China over its Most Favoured Nation status became all the more embarrassing as human rights violations in Tibet and China rapidly worsened. As HRW concludes, 'increasingly human rights' are being seen 'less as a dispensable luxury and more as an essential underpinning to global well-being'. One of the principal targets for the human rights movement today is to attack the reign of 'commercial diplomacy', which allows economic interests to dominate foreign policy, and to challenge World Bank and multinational corporation complicity in abuses. Royal Dutch Shell's refusal, in Nigeria, to engage in anything more biting than 'quiet diplomacy' over the military attacks on the Ogoni people, or the execution of Ken Saro-Wiwa, has left what HRW calls a 'dark stain on its reputation'.

A S REFLECTED in these annual reports, 1995 was a year in which calls for an international system of justice, and an international criminal court, grew more insistent. While Judge Goldstone has been battling against the tepid commitment of governments to his tribunal for those guilty of war crimes in Bosnia and Rwanda, throughout Latin America there have been signs that the public is determined to see some of the main perpetrators of the continent's 'dirty wars' bought to trial. 'Only justice', concludes HRW, 'can establish the rule of law to replace the cycle of summary revenge.' For both Bosnia and Rwanda, justice, seen to be done, has taken on enormous significance. The Dayton peace agreement in November made some progress by banning indicted war criminals from holding office, but the same resolve to back a tough legal stand has not been forthcoming in Rwanda, where 57,000 people suspected of genocidal crimes await trials that can never take place unless the rest of the world provides money and manpower. All but a handful of Tutsi magistrates and lawyers were murdered during the massacres. President Clinton has gone so far as to endorse the idea of a permanent court, but then seriously weakened the whole concept by agreeing to Security Council approval before any prosecution can take place.

And for all the stirrings of public conscience, there is not yet much to applaud. If 1994 is remembered for the mutilated bodies piled one upon the other in Rwanda, no scene is more evocative of the violence of 1995 than that of the 8,000 Muslim men and boys led away to execution by their Serbian captors before the eyes of UN peacekeepers. The story of the war in former Yugoslavia, and the response of the rest of the world, is told in Michele Mercier's *Crimes without Punishment*. It did nothing to boost respect for the UN's humanitarian actions, already brought low by its cowardice and indecision in Somalia and Rwanda. Though human rights issues now dominate the day-to-day agenda of the Security Council, few of these concerns are translated into effective action. The UN high commissioner for human rights, Jose Ayala Lasso, continues to be timid in his dealings with abusive regimes, and his voice is not heard in UN Security Council debates.

Among Amnesty International's concerns in 1995 has been an insidious variant of the 'ethnic cleansing' that became infamous in Bosnia. Known as 'social cleansing' in Colombia, this takes the form of clean-up operations by death squads of people considered 'disposable' — homosexuals, prostitutes, drug addicts, vagrants, street children and the

MARTIN ADLER/PANOS PICTURES

Rwanda 1994: 'few human rights issues are translated into action'

mentally retarded. The killers, operating from motorcycles and the backs of trucks are often employed by local shopkeepers, driven to murder by years of unchecked urban crime. Hundreds of people, says AI, are now dying at the hands of these shadowy hired gunmen every year. In nearby Brazil, lynch mobs have taken over the solving of petty crime. When the bodies turn up, they show signs of castration and mutilation.

It is now 18 months since the Beijing women's conference, when 2,000 delegates from 189 countries descended on China to reaffirm a declaration that women's rights are now to be regarded as an 'inalienable, integral and indivisible part of human rights'. Human Rights Watch's *Global Report on Women's Rights*, while pointing to a forceful surge in interest and determination among women to break through the barriers of silence and censorship that continue to shroud most acts of violence perpetrated 'nst them, nonetheless presents a somewhat dismal pattern. Rape, /hether during wars, in prison or in refugee camps, remains for the most part unreported and seldom prosecuted; in many parts of southeast Asia, the active involvement of border guards and police in the trafficking of women and girls for forced prostitution is rarely questioned; and it is still true that in 1995, as in all preceding years, there is virtually no country in the world in which domestic violence is not the main cause of female injury. ❏

Caroline Moorehead is a writer and broadcaster specialising in human rights

Reporters sans Frontières, 1995 Report *and updates; IPI* 1995 World Press Freedom Review; *Committee to Protect Journalists, 1995-6; Human Rights Watch* Global Report on Women's Human Rights; *Amnesty International* 1995 Report *with updates; ICRC reports on* Blinding Weapons *and* Landmines, 1995; Crimes without punishment. Humanitarian action in the former Yugoslavia, *Michele Mercier, Pluto Press*